A Turbulent Life

Jock Nicolson

Published by Praxis Press

Acknowledgements

So many people have been involved in producing this book that it is not possible to name all of them but special mention must be made of Penny Borrow, David Berkovitch, Jose Nicolson and Louise Nicolson-Ellis.

Thanks are also due to The London Museum and Henry Grant for some of the photographs.

Praxis Press would like to thank and acknowledge the generous support of the RMT - the National Union of Rail, Maritime and Transport Workers – and the family of Jock Nicolson for their assistance in publishing this book.

A Turbulent Life
Jock Nicolson

ISBN: 978-1-899155-04-0

Published and distributed by
Praxis Press
Unity Books
72 Waterloo Street
Glasgow G2, Scotland, UK
Tel: +44 141 204 1611
Email: praxispress@mac.com

Contents

FOREWORD

It was a privilege to know Jock Nicolson. He was a life-long class fighter and trade-union activist as well as being very funny and engaging man.

His early experiences of poverty led him to become an effective poacher to feed his family, acutely class-conscious and a well-read socialist.

His generation lived through the rise of fascism in Spain and Germany, but Jock was one of the many that decided to do something about it by agitating and educating working people about the dangers of the Nazi menace.

Wherever Jock was, he always exerted a huge political influence and helped develop and spread socialist ideas.

When not involved in rent strikes or standing as a Communist Party candidate in London, Jock was a great host and many an activist enjoyed his social gatherings at his home with his wife Bridget.

You may have disagreed with Jock on some things, but you could always discuss differences in a comradely manner. His oratorical skills came to the fore during his two terms on the executive of National Union of Railwaymen, where he always upheld and defended the democratic structures of the union.

He was a thorn in the flesh of any trade union leader, including in the NUR, if they didn't lead and defend workers. Jock was fiercely proud of his class and understood the vicious nature of the boss class. He taught us younger activists that in order to win a better deal for working people you must be prepared to fight when necessary and cajole where possible.

It is a lesson we forget at our peril.

Bob Crow
General Secretary, RMT

Chapter 1 - Burnt Porridge

The two decades before the Second World War was a very unhappy time for thousands of families in Hamilton. Unemployment was high and housing conditions primitive.

For many years our family lived in a one-room flat in a large tenement building. At the far end of the room under the window was a cold-water tap over a cast-iron sink, with a small draining board attached. The door was at the other end of the room and next to it there was a bed-in-the-wall. There was an open fireplace half-way along one of the walls with hobs at either side. That is where the kettles were kept hot and the porridge made — and often burned — when my mother's attention was distracted with one household chore or another. There was a gas cooker near the fire with an ordinary bed directly opposite on the other wall.

All the household paraphernalia, baths, buckets, baskets of dirty clothing, etc., were crammed underneath the beds. This one overcrowded room was the total accommodation for both parents and four boys and one girl, ranging from the baby to teenagers. The two elder boys and the baby slept with their head to the foot of the bed-in-the-wall with the parents laying the opposite way. I slept with my sister in the other bed. When my father was working he did three shifts, including nights, so that he had to get his sleep during the day. This imposed a strict and unnatural discipline of quietness on the children. It was quite a strain.

Once a week my mother had to get down on her knees and scrub the floor. Everyone had to clear out for this major operation. Chairs were piled on top of the table and beds then moved from one end of the room to the other as she progressed. For me, not yet at school, this was a terribly disturbing experience. My little world was turned upside down. It upset me so much that I got to know the washing day of every housewife in the tenement. I used to look in and urge them to finish quickly. The psychological impact was so deep that even to this day I cannot bear to see a thread on the floor and make myself a bloody nuisance with the vacuum cleaner all day long.

The cast-iron sink was where everyone washed. There was the same ritual every night for us children. We were stood in the sink naked and one by one washed from head to feet by mother. If she was in a good mood we might get some hot water from the kettle added to the tap water to take off the chill. Even then the cold draught from the poorly fitting window made this an operation that was dreaded. When the wash was completed there was a compulsory pee in the sink so that we would not have to get up for it during the night. As soon as that was over there was a rush to get in front of the coal fire, which in spite of our poverty was always heaped up and glowing red.

Another fear that was often on our minds was about the burned porridge. If you have ever thrown woollen socks on a fire then that is exactly the smell and taste of burned porridge, sometimes this happened when mother's attention was diverted. Naturally, she would be furious about the accident and, in her anger, would still put it in front of us although she knew we would go to school on an empty belly rather than swallow that nauseating stuff. If the morning had gone badly for mother, we might even get that cold burned porridge when we came home for our mid-day meal. By that time it would have a covering of thick skin, which made it more disgusting and unpalatable. Invariably mother surrendered to our continuing resistance but we would have to be satisfied with a jeely piece instead of the hot soup or tatties and mince which we would have relished.

When I was still small we moved from Johnston Street to a two-roomed flat also in a large tenement. By our standards it was a big improvement as far as accommodation goes. But it certainly was no paradise, for we were directly opposite the great waste heap of the old Bent Colliery. One of my abiding memories of this flat was the sour smell when there was a lot of rain and the walls became damp. In those days it was the practice to stick on wallpaper with ordinary flour paste and in those old houses there was layer after layer on the walls. It was said that that was what held the building up as there was so much shifting from the disused mine workings underneath. Anyway the smell was so unpleasant that I swore never to have wallpaper in any house I might have in the future.

Much later, just after the outbreak of the Second World War, we were moved to a completely new council house with all the modern conveniences. But it was a bit late, for by that time my father was dead and one brother after another was called up to defend our great heritage! My father had married quite late in life, when I was still a child he had retired at 70 years of age from the railway and was not in good health. He had a small railway pension and the state pension of 10 shillings a week. This was not enough to keep seven people.

My oldest brother worked as an errand boy, but even we children were expected to make some contribution. Our family qualified for Parish Relief. This meant that once a year the children were supplied with a suit and a pair of boots. Collecting them was a terribly frightening experience for my mother. The issuing officer was a bullying creature, who bawled and shouted at parents and children. Some time later he was jailed on a petty embezzlement charge connected with his job. He was a First World War casualty, having had one of his legs blown off, so he didn't have such a wonderful life either.

One of the consequences of this Parish Relief makes me blush with embarrassment even to this day. My mother made us children go to St. John's Church on Sundays and, as these Parish boots were heavy and hob nailed, we could be heard clop, clop, clop along the wooden gallery to the furthest point where our pew was. That was a loud and clear declaration that we were Parish children. What shame and humiliation we felt.

One sin I committed at that time troubled me so much that I can still remember it 70 years later. Mother gave me two pennies; one was for the collection in church and the other for the Sunday school that followed straight after. But for weeks I had been sorely tempted. A large bar of Cadbury's milk chocolate was two pence. I had never had one and that Sunday the temptation was too much and I couldn't resist any longer. Skipping church and Sunday school did not worry me. It was the thought that I had cheated my mother that weighed on my mind for a long time afterwards.

The reason my mother made us go to church every Sunday didn't have very much to do with the Bible or religious devotion. It was a kind of demonstrative act, like holding up a banner that said: 'We might be poor but we are still part of the respectable section of the community'. That is how many Protestant working-class women felt. Long-term unemployment and low wages had taken their toll and they no longer had Sunday finery to wear so they rarely went to church themselves but by God they sent their children just to prove to themselves and everyone else that they were still respectable. Somehow we children came to think of the Catholics as being of a lower order than us. Their Sunday ended at mid-day then they could enjoy themselves for the rest of the day; the old ones gathering at the street corner and the children playing football in the back yard. Not so for us Protestants. We had to remain solemn the whole day. There is little doubt that the Protestant community was more class-ridden than the Catholics.

The Catholics were mostly of Irish extraction and Sunday morning Mass was really a coming together of their entire community, whereas Protestant congregations were made up mainly from professional and business people and their families. They appeared to have a higher social standing than Protestant manual workers. This was even more obvious with the women with their fine clothing and genteel postures. It turned many working men away from the church.

Naturally, some of this attitude was carried over into the Sunday school. I remember being sent to a Sunday school summer camp in the Highlands when I was about eight or nine years old. There was only one other boy apart from myself who came from a poor family. We had been nominated and paid for by some church charity. I was very conscious of this and felt miserable the whole time. It was not that any of the other children even hinted at our situation. They were far too well brought up to do so; rather it was that they were so good mannered, well-spoken and self-confident that I felt completely out of my depth. This was the first time I had been away from my own family and from the rough, tough tenement environment. I felt miserable the whole time. I remember it as one of the longest and most tormented weeks of my life.

The next village to ours, about two miles away, was Blantyre, the birthplace of the famous African explorer and missionary David Livingstone. He was lost in the jungle for many months and Stanley, another explorer, went in search of him. A miracle happened. They bumped into each other in the middle of a thicket. "Doctor Livingstone, I presume," said Stanley as they politely shook hands as though it was a commonplace encounter. Every child in Scotland has been told that story a hundred times, and never tired of it. What an adventure! So different from the solemn old men in serge suits and polished boots with a Bible in one hand and umbrella in the other that we met on Sundays making their way to church.

When I grew a bit older I refused to go to church and became an atheist and spouted all the anti-religious arguments. We often said that the imperialists went with a gun in one hand and a Bible in the other. But today, on mature reflection, I feel grateful for some of the ideas I absorbed in the church. The Church of Scotland had many missionaries in Africa and the stories we were told by them implanted a deep feeling of humanism and compassion for these poor black children who suffered much worse from poverty and disease than we knew. Strange as it may seem, I think it was these religious humanist teachings that prepared the ground for my conversion to communism.

For us, there was never any question of a week's holiday by the seaside. Sometimes there would be a one-day outing. Personally I can only remember one such occasion. My father took two of us to see the Falls of Leni near Callender. I cannot recall that we actually saw that famous beauty spot. All I remember is that we got a German biscuit in the baker's shop in Callender where there was quite an argument about the correct name for the biscuit. Apparently before the First World War it was called a German biscuit, then patriotism decreed that the name should be changed to Empire biscuit, and as my father was not a 'King and Country' man he had used the old title, hence the row.

During the long school holidays in summer my mother might take us to the river Avon, a mile away, for a picnic. This was regarded as something very special. In the main we were left to our own devices and we never found it a problem to fill in time and enjoy ourselves. There were games such as skitie. This was played with the lovely coloured cards you used to get in cigarette packets. You had to flick your cards against a wall and try and cover one of your opponents's to win all that had been played. Another amusement was girrs and kleiks (hoops). You had races with them, imagining you were a racing car. A blacksmith would make you a heavy one called a wind-cheater for a copper or two. I remember one of these went through a shop window and in a flash every boy in the street had dissolved into thin air. Then there were peeries (spinning tops). The test was to see how long you could keep them upright. The girls played peever (hop scotch) with a used Cherry Blossom shoe polish tin and peever beds chalked out on the pavement. In my 40 years in London, I've not seen that game played once. Then there were skipping rope games. No self-respecting boy would be seen at this, but secretly we admired and envied the rubber knee joints these girls must have had.

There must have been a cruel streak in my makeup. We had an old-fashioned pram with very big wheels and a well-sprung body. We would give my sister Ruthie a ride in it up the Low Waters Brae then when we got to the top I would run as fast as I could down hill and let it go. Ruthie would be somersaulted into the air when it crashed. She never clyped (told on us). How could I do such a thing to Ruthie who had always been so kind to me? It is something I cannot explain. I hope I've made amends since. Of course we were naughty. Some of us would stow-away on a train into Glasgow. In preparation for the trip we would have placed some metal beer bottle tops on the tram lines. If you were lucky they would be flattened the exact size of a penny. They could be used in the station slot machine where you could get one big fat Churchman No. 1 cigarette in its own individual packet. Otherwise you would smoke cinnamon stick if you could keep it alight, and then finish eating it. It has quite a pleasant taste.

The attraction in Glasgow was the railway horses. They were enormous Clydesdales with legs like oak trees. A pilot horse and drayman would be stationed at the bottom of the steeper streets to assist with the heavy loads. Quite often a horse would fall. It wouldn't be able to get up because the shafts held it rigid, and the drayman would have to undo the harness. The moment the horse felt itself free it would heave up on its hind legs with forelegs thrashing the air. In an instant the drayman would have to throw himself to the side. They were great big men just like their horses. What an exciting sight. Who needed a circus when all this was real — and free into the bargain!

I cannot remember whether we received pocket money when we were children. If we did it was very little. When I was seven or eight years old I used to do the Saturday morning shopping for an old lady who lived further down our street. She had the annoying habit of sending me to the far end of the town, about half a mile walk, to the pork butcher; then when I returned she would give me another errand to a shop next to that butcher. She seemed to think that a child's mind should not be overburdened with complex instructions. When the shopping was completed – it would take about three hours – she would wrap two pennies in a large wad of newspaper; that was for my mother, and another penny wrapped and carefully deposited in my pocket; that was my pocket money.

One of the items I had to get every week for the old lady was cow's liver. Her daughter was anaemic and the doctor had prescribed liver, chopped up and eaten raw, as a medicine. I think that many medical practitioners at that time were a cross between animal vets and witch doctors. They all had their own favourite incantations. I remember my mother taking me to our doctor one time when my face became all spotty with pimples. The doctor had an enormous belly, so big that when he stretched his arms over it, only the finger-tips touched. He gave one look at me and snapped "His food is too rich. No more sugar in his tea." I suppose I was lucky he didn't suggest blood-letting. Even though I was only a child, I thought it was quite rich for old fat-guts to deprive me of one of the foods I liked very much.

Actually, there might have been something in the doctor's remedy. One of the consequences of us not getting sweets or cake was that we did use sugar to excess. One of my favourite food items was a slice of white bread liberally spread with margarine then sprinkled thickly with sugar. The sugar was worked in by a back and forward movement of the knife till it had a cream-like constituency. Another common substitute for sweeties was a stalk of rhubarb dipped into a poke of sugar. Children in the street enjoying rhubarb and sugar were as frequent a sight then as children with their bag of crisps today.

There were two special days when practically every child could expect to get a penny from mother. That was when the 'gas man' came to empty the penny-in-the-slot gas meter, and when the co-op dividend was collected. The 'gas man' was easily identified. He had a Gladstone bag for carrying the pennies and walked with a very straight back but leaning over slightly to one side to counter-balance the weight in his bag. When he appeared in your street he was spotted immediately and trailed till he arrived at your house. There was always a rebate. The pennies were piled on the table in columns of 12 to make a shilling, and when the counting was completed so many columns would be swept into the Gladstone bag with a great flourish of the 'gas man's' hand, and the remainder left for mother. This was a breath-taking sight, like a magician's trick at the circus, especially as you knew that one of these pennies would end up burning a hole in your pocket.

The Co-op dividend was a much more serious business. The 'divi' was an important contribution to the family income, and was ear-marked well in advance for the more expensive household necessities such as boots or clothes for the winter. The receipt for every transaction in the co-op was a small piece of paper about two inches by three, which showed your share number and the value of your purchases. My mother filed every one of these slips on a wire. When the dividend was declared, and it could be half a crown in the pound or more, she would spend an evening adding up the receipts and calculating how much she could expect. She was never far out.

We started by talking about the old lady in our street who I did the shopping for. She was shattered by a tragic accident to her only grandchild, a little boy of four or five who lived with her son and his wife in the flat underneath her. The boy's dad worked in the gasworks just a hundred yards away at the foot of our street. Every day at mid-day the little boy used to run down with his dad's lunch box. It was quite moving to see them rushing into each other's arms. Then one day as the child was running to meet his dad he was caught by the wire hawser that pulled the coal wagons into the gasworks, and in a flash both his legs were amputated. It happened so quickly that nothing could be done. Fate can be so cruel and irrational. That is how the whole street felt.

Although our house was only 20 yards away from the school gates and I grew up alongside it, I did not enjoy a single day of my schooling. In fact I hated school even before I was old enough to be a pupil. At that tender age, school was associated with noise, disorder and conflict. Just imagine a few hundred children ranging from 5 years of age to 14 all being released from the discipline of the classroom for their 10-minute break. It was called playtime. Some played football, others ran races, a few engaged in fisticuffs, and everyone shouting and screaming at top pitch. It was Bedlam. And that was what I witnessed every school day from a few yards away.

All the mothers in the street had children at the school and at playtime they would gather in little groups nearby. They pretended to themselves that they were keeping an eye on their offspring's, but in reality it was the first communal gossip of the day. Many scandals were exposed and reputations ruined in these ten minutes. But occasionally mums had to perform rescue operations. Sometimes a child would push his head through the railings and if he had big ears that stuck out at right angles he would get caught like a fish is caught in a net by the gills. He would panic, wriggle and become even more firmly imprisoned and hysterical. But the mums had seen all that happen before. They knew exactly what to do: pacify the child, pin him between their powerful knees, and then gently manoeuvre the head back, one ear at a time.

I can actually remember my first day at school. I was sat on a bench alongside a boy called Robert Bruce. Soon I felt my buttocks getting warm. It was quite a comfortable feeling at first till I realised that Robert had wet himself and it had run along the bench to me. He had been too timid to ask to be excused and I was too wary to say anything about it, so both of us suffered in silence. I think Robert must have been a descendant of that great historical figure Robert the Bruce of spider fame, for he developed into a great big hulk of a boy. If ever I was being roughed up by some bully Robert would turn up by my side; he was a kind of guardian angel to me. That wet bench on our first day at school had somehow cemented our relations.

It is well known that the Scots are mad on football. During the summer holidays it was the most popular game. It was played in the street and often a window would be broken and the game would be prohibited for some time. But it always came back. I never really liked the game, mainly because I could never kick the ball straight. There was a small group like me who said they were interested in 'nature'. We would go up to the forest and look for nests or fish for minnows or tadpoles in the ponds.

On one of these expeditions I climbed over the spiked iron railings in Auchingramont Road and on my return one foot caught between the spikes. The next second, I was swinging head down with my left leg bent forward into an inverted 'U'. I looked up at the horribly distorted flesh and bone then fainted. By good luck a young man witnessed this from just a few yards away. He was going to a First Aid class and knew how to lift me off with the minimum of damage.

I spent the next month in the Royal Infirmary in Glasgow. When I was told I had a broken leg I understood this to mean that I only had one and a half legs now. I couldn't see anything. I was strapped to the bed with a cage over my damaged leg, and it was only when I had great pain in my non-existent foot that an examination was made and I discovered that the leg had not broken off completely. In fact the foot was now double the size it used to be. The plaster had been too tight and had affected the circulation. That was not the end. The bone had not been properly set and had to be broken and done all over again, that month was one of the longest and most anguished periods of my childhood. I thought for most of the time that I would be a cripple for life. Even getting visitors did not assuage my anxiety. The only pleasant thing I remember was when someone brought me in a snow cake. This was a sponge with jam in the middle and icing sprinkled with coconut on top. We never had such luxuries at home.

I don't see these cakes nowadays. If I did, I would buy one and give it to the first unhappy child I came across as a thanksgiving token.

8

Chapter 2 – With God and Nature

Social attitudes in the 1930s were very different from today. Children then were acutely class-conscious. We thought of teachers as being above us: a kind of upper class. In all honesty, I think teachers saw themselves in that way too. One of them who sticks in my mind was old Granny McCulloch. She was an old Highland lady and I suppose still had the Laird complex in her being. Anyway she never tired of telling us that the rich had as big a burden to carry as the poor. One day I reported this to my mother. She told me: "The next time Miss McCulloch comes out with that tell her I'm quite prepared to shoulder their burden." Soon the occasion arose to do this. I can still see that lady marching up the corridor in fury and smacking my face. What injustice, what humiliation, for saying something in complete innocence. I think it was that incident that started the process of sensitivity being turned into combative class-consciousness.

But life is full of strange quirks. I was about 11 years old at this time and fell madly in love for the first time – and who would it be but granny McCulloch's niece! I followed her everywhere. Soon this engaged the attention of the old lady. She was furious and seemed to think of it as a challenge to the death. Soon her opportunity was to come. I imagine all children coming near their teens feel very superior if they can tell smutty stories – even if they only half understand them. It so happened there was one of these being circulated in our class at this time. It was a piece of paper which said something like this: "Mary Marshall laundress etc. etc. and when it was folded over it read: "Mary shall undress at 10 pm, trousers down at..."

Somehow old Granny McCulloch got hold of it. She went to the headmaster and presented it as though the morals of the entire school were being undermined. Unfortunately, Isaac Lightbody, the head, already had a very sour view of humanity. He made us feel that we were thoroughly evil and unworthy people and would never ever make decent human beings. After such a savage dressing down I didn't have a very high regard for myself for a long time. Looking back, I think it was the teachers who should have felt ashamed for so undermining a child's self respect.

Johnny C, another teacher was quite a different character. Normally, he was gentle and good-natured but at times he would start throwing any object that came to hand at the pupils. There was no hostility from parents. Johnny had been in the trenches in the First World War and was a serious shell-shock casualty. Parents knew that was the reason for his unpredictable behaviour, and their compassion rubbed off onto the unfortunate pupils who were sometimes his victims. The war and depression certainly damaged the lives and personality of very many people. I must refer here to another teacher: Elizabeth Marlin, a middle-aged spinster who taught French. She was rather strict, and as this was a subject that I was neither interested in nor could master, we would probably have forgotten each other's existence very soon. She carried on some charitable activities and I can remember her coming to our door on one occasion when I was positively rude to her. Some years later, when she had retired and I was the secretary of the Hamilton branch of the Communist Party, she joined the Party. She became the secretary of the Scotland–USSR Society, turning it into a very highly respected body, which for many years afterwards played quite an important role in developing cultural links between our two countries.

The last story I want to tell about teachers concerns Miss Dick. What made her notable was the fact that she was the fiancée of a well-known footballer. She had the unnerving habit of looking over your shoulder at your exercise and making comments. "Jock," she said, "you are brainless." "Well miss," I replied, "it's better to be brainless than have nae brains at 'a!"

At school I was never very interested in games like football. In fact, in all my life I've only been at a football match twice, and that was during the war to take a collection for medical aid to Russia. I was much more interested in nature. I think I got this through Alec, my elder brother. He kept birds and we used to go out together with lime or trap nets to catch the finches he wanted for hybrid breeding. I graduated from that to rabbit catching. By the time I had left school I already had some ferrets. Rabbits became an important part of our family's diet and supplemented our income. If I took rabbits to the butcher on a Thursday I would get 6d for a full-grown one. On Saturday it was only 4d on the grounds that he might not be able to sell them before the weekend. I also became interested in fishing through my closest school friend, Alec Crawford, who lived in the next close to us. His father was an accomplished angler and when he caught scores of wee trout my mother would get a dozen or so on the understanding that she would keep it quiet as they were not the required eight inches take-able size.

The rivers Avon and Clyde were less than a mile away from our home and we boys spent much of the summer holidays fishing there for perch, which were easy to catch. Our equipment was primitive, consisting of a big garden cane and a halfpenny hook. The line was an ordinary piece of string coated with candle grease to make it waterproof. The other thing that we were passionate about, especially while we were at the lower end of the age scale, was the cinema. The Saturday matinee cost only 1d, and if you didn't have that much, there was a little shop next door where you could get the 1d for a couple of empty jam jars. At Gilchrist's factory nearby you could get an enormous bag of broken biscuits or crumbs also for 1d. What a treat that provided for a whole gang of us on a Saturday afternoon. *Tarzan the Ape Man* was one of the serials that captured us most. At the end of each episode, he would be falling into a snake pit or alligator infested river to almost certain death. That would keep us in suspense for the whole week until the following instalment. Equally popular were the Wild West films. When the baddie crept up behind the goodie and was about to pull the trigger the entire audience would be on its feet: "look round, look round, look round!" What excitement, what involvement! Does anything like that happen in the cinema today?

Spring was the time for collecting bird's eggs. Most of the boys concentrated on the hedgerows for the eggs of the smaller birds and made up sets of the different breeds. I went for the bigger ones that we could eat at home. If I got plenty they would be shared with the neighbours. I don't know if you have ever tasted a wild bird's egg? How different, what flavour. By just thinking about it, I know that my boiled battery egg tomorrow morning will look and taste like congealed cotton wool. The Peewits are amongst the earliest layers. I have always thought of them as very stupid birds. They don't conceal their nests or build them high up on the inaccessible branches of trees. They simply lay their clutch of four eggs in any indent in the short grass or even on newly ploughed bare earth. They must have company; they cannot stand being on their own, so you can find dozens of nests in one field. All you need to do is to walk up and down the field a few paces apart each time and soon you will have as many eggs as you can carry home. I always felt a bit uneasy about this. True, they were lazy and stupid birds, but what a plaintive call they made when you robbed them of their next generation. The water birds, moorhens, coots, ducks, etc., were numerous in the ponds and marches alongside the Clyde and Avon and their nests were easy to find. When you came across a nest you would put one egg in the water and if it sank to the bottom it was fresh enough to take. When it floated that meant that the chick inside had begun to develop and you left that nest alone.

I have come to learn that the one British bird you need to be afraid of is the swan, not the eagle. I learned that lesson when I robbed a swan's nest in the Hough Park that runs alongside the Motherwell Road. I was 11 or 12 years of age at the time. The nest was on a raised tussock about ten yards inside the pond. I took off my boots and stockings and rolled up the legs of my short trousers and waded in. A couple of yards from the nest, the water went a bit deeper so I took off my trousers as well and laid them on some nearby rushes that were above water level. By this time I got to the nest both male and female birds were rearing and jabbing at me with their long necks and open beaks, hissing all the time.

It became a bit alarming but I did manage to get two of the eggs and made my way back to dry land as quick as I could. By this time both birds had gone berserk, flapping and beating at me with their enormous wings. I had to run for it with the swans following me and kicking up an almighty row. Then it dawned on me that I had no trousers; they were lying there alongside the swans' nest. What was I to do? It struck me immediately that it was God punishing me for stealing the Queen of birds' eggs. I knew I had to accept some kind of punishment, but surely not the humiliation of having to walk through the town without trousers. There is nothing better for sharpening the wits than such a situation. I set down the two stolen eggs on a hummock of grass. This seemed to confuse the swans for they forgot me and fussed around the eggs.

I was off in a flash, made a detour back to my trousers by the nest, grabbed the two remaining eggs that I hadn't managed to get before, and made a bee line in the opposite direction while the swans were still puzzling what to do with the landlocked ones so far away from the water. By the time I got home and sitting down to egg pancake I felt quite cocky again. Not only had I deceived the swans but I had put one over on God as well, and not many people can do that.

Not far from that scene I had another watery adventure a little later that summer. I was fishing for perch where the banking was quite high above a deep run of fast water. I must have been dreaming when suddenly off went the line with a whiz. I suppose it was the excitement, but it caused me to overbalance and into the water I went still holding on to my rod – I wasn't going to lose that no matter what happened. When I did clamber out I had a nice pike at the end of the line. It weighed about a couple of pounds, and for me in those days that was a real whopper that made the soaking a mere detail.

There was a belief among some of our people that the pike was an 'unclean' fish and should not be eaten. They were thought to be cannibal fish. Horrifying stories were told of the corpses of drowned people being hauled out of the river with practically all their flesh eaten away by pike. And, as some of the corpses were suicides, it was said that if you ate the pike you were something of a cannibal yourself and might even become infected with the depression that drove the suicide to a watery end. Still, I was too proud of my monster fish to allow that to worry me at the time. I ate it. I can recommend pike as a great delicacy. It had a firm white flaky flesh that comes off the bones easier than that of most other fish. And I am fairly certain that the depression that I sometimes suffer from these days has nothing to do with that wonderful meal I had 60 years ago.

You will have noticed that I talk a lot about food. This is not because I, or anyone in our community, went hungry as many millions in the Third World do today. True, our diet was monotonous. Breakfast was always porridge made from rough oats and water. Soup two or three times a week made from a big marrow bone and laced with plenty of roots, peas and lentils. The third meal was always tea, bread and marge spread with jam or treacle. We didn't get many salads, and I notice even today when I am holidaying in Scotland greens are not all that easy to come by. Anyway, the usual cry of a child when he came home from school was "Maw 'am starvin! Gimme a jeely piece" and shortly both cheeks right to the ears were sticky with dust and grime.

In later years when I had become an accomplished poacher, we had rabbit at least once a week in the winter; that was before the myxomatosis disease. When I was working alongside Alec he bet me a sixpence that I couldn't eat the whole rabbit that was in the pot on top of the heap of potatoes on my plate. We had no more than half an hour for our meal then we had to rush back to work. I scoffed the lot, but he never paid me because I had left a teaspoonful of gravy in the bottom of the pot.

In the summer the coal merchant across the road from us used to scrub his coal float, scatter some grass on it, and use it for selling herring round the streets. In these days herring were plentiful in the Firth of Clyde; now it is the Polaris subs that are there and the herring have disappeared. One year there was such a glut of herring that the Salvation Army brought trainloads of them to Hamilton Station Yard and distributed them free. At first the women and children collected them on plates. Then they became bolder and fetched them in basins and some in the two-handed zinc baths that tenement dwellers used for washing in. You can imagine the smell of frying herring in every nook and cranny of all the tenements when every family was preparing dinner. Later on this was replaced with a vinegar smell when pickling was the only way to deal with such a bountiful and free harvest. I mentioned the coal merchant. Today he would be described as an entrepreneur just like Margaret Thatcher's old man. Rubbish, he was more likely to be a half-crippled miner or building worker who couldn't stick the pace. The one I'm thinking of had a horse so old and weak that he had to get the help of some of us to lift it up each morning.

I've already mentioned old man Crawford. From time to time he would go on the booze. On one such night, when he was staggering all over the place, he was picked up by one of the local bobbies, a Constable Callighan. Our street was part of Callighan's beat and, whenever he set foot in it, we children would abandon our games or whatever we were doing and quietly disappear. It was his grim and forbidding countenance that frightened us. But he couldn't have been all that bad for instead of taking old Sanny to the cells to sober up, he took him home and said he would call for him the following morning. That is how Sanny became involved with a religious sect which had premises called the Olive Hall in the next street to ours. For a few weeks, old Sanny, instead of going to the pub every Saturday night, would be a street corner-preacher. He would stand with a Bible in one hand and the other one pointing heavenward and shout slogans in a very loud voice like: "Join us in the Olive Hall, be washed in the blood of the lamb and saved from eternal damnation!" All this was a bit incomprehensible to me and a bit frightening as well, for I had often seen old Sanny wringing a rabbit's neck, and this blood of a lamb must have been from one that he had knocked off on the way home from a fishing expedition. Being Sanny's son's best friend, I was inveigled against my will into attending some of the Saturday night sessions in the Olive Hall. I didn't see any blood. Instead, I was given a cup of tea and a bun and declared 'saved'. Nevertheless, I always felt uneasy singing songs of praise to the Lord. I knew within myself that I was insincere. Our Presbyterian religion had frightening overtones. It was everywhere and permeated everything. Walking in the country you would suddenly encounter a painted slogan 'FLEE FROM THE WRATH TO COME!' I often had a real fear that the world was about to come to an end. It had the psychological effect of giving us a morose disposition. 'Dour Boots' we are called, and with some justification.

In spite of rather dreary domestic circumstances and my dislike of sport, I think of my childhood as being interesting and exciting. All my companions were of a like kind. We imagined ourselves as hunters or explorers. We knew every tree and blade of grass for miles around: the High Parks, Ross Estate, Quarter, Limekiln burn, Earnock Muir, etc. If it wasn't sabre-toothed tigers that chased us it was equally ferocious farmers or gamekeepers. We made fires and stewed strong black tea in Billy cans, fried minnows, and on one occasion tried to bake a hedgehog in clay the way we had read about in a book.

There was quite a literature of that kind for boys and we tried all the tricks suggested including catching pheasants by blinding them by flashlight while they were perching in the dark. One experiment we wanted to try but which was out of our reach was soaking oats in whisky for the pheasants and waiting till they were so drunk that you could take them by hand. We did come across old poachers who had tried out that experiment on themselves!

I know that deprivation still exists, but one thing that strikes me today is that children of the poor appear to be clean and quite well dressed. I know that when we were children this was not the case. Our top clothing at least, and stockings, were invariably dirty and smelly – and sometimes even lousy. What boy didn't have shiny sleeves from wiping his nose? This was because washing machines had not yet been invented and tenement families usually got only one day a fortnight in the communal washhouse. Yet I have never seen a social study that has given these machines credit for the physical and social uplift they have given to the poor. Where is the modern poet who will immortalise them?

Women were the worst victims of the depression years. The hopelessness of the situation had led many of them to stop caring about their appearance or their health. I'm thinking at the moment of one of our next-door neighbours. She was by no means one of the worst-off. Her husband was a plasterer and in good weather had decent spells of work. They once had a week's holiday in Northern Ireland – which was not very common. But in winter there were often long spells of unemployment because of the frost. At the time I'm thinking of, Nan would have been in her mid-30s. I can still see her; thin as a rake and lantern-jawed. She would be at the close-mouth gathering of the women, competing with one another about how many aspirins they had already taken that morning to get rid of their headache. Other women were grotesquely obese, also because they had stopped caring. Another picture I have in my mind: a blazing hot day and a crowd of women sitting down in the drying green behind the tenement; a blouse is opened and an enormous balloon of bosom drops out for the baby to suckle as I pass by. It strikes me – a sensitive young boy – as obscene and I avert my eyes.

Still, real life is strange. The fattest woman I have ever seen was Teena McC, who lived in our tenement. She was so blown up that the fat of her ankles hung over her shoes and scraped the ground. Her husband – and she used to boast about it – was the ugliest man on God's earth. Yet they were probably the happiest couple in our little community. No doubt this was because he was a miner in regular work and they had no children, so they were not crushed down by poverty as most of the others were. The other group of unfortunates were the unemployed young men. Many of them had not worked since they had left school and it looked as though there was very little prospect of their position ever improving. They hung around the street corner most of the day looking dejected and apathetic. They didn't get a lot of sympathy from some who were more fortunate and dubbed them as 'corner boys' who didn't want to work. A few years later when the war started these very same 'corner boys' were working 12 hours a day seven days a week.

In the inter-war years quite a number of people from our area had emigrated to Canada in search of work. But the depression was worldwide and things were no better there and welfare services were even worse than they were at home. These families started coming back in dribs and drabs, telling distressing stories of others who were unable to afford their passage home. Sometimes street collections were taken to help them. I can remember one family coming home. The whole street turned out to welcome them; a very moving demonstration of community solidarity it was.

Nowadays – and I am writing this at the beginning of 1992 – I think back to the pre-war depression. Yes, it was a truly depressing time. But I think today's unemployment is even worse, at least in the big cities like London. In Hamilton in the 30s the unemployed were part of the community. The young men might have hung around the street corners looking mindless and dejected. But they had relatives and were not allowed to sink too far. The relatives, and the community generally, acted as some kind of social support and a restraint against their total deterioration. Ironically, when the war came they found work and very soon had their pride and self-respect restored. But what you have in London today is different. The unemployed drifters have no connection with any local community not only men, but women as well, and increasingly, young girls too.

You get to recognise particular individuals. You can see them slide from hopelessness to depravity, whining and begging for the price of a can of beer. And I'm talking about those who gather in little groups in the main thoroughfares; so far they have exercised enough self-control to keep away from the notorious vice areas. But have they already gone too far to rehabilitate themselves? What a horrible price they are paying in loss of human dignity for our return to a full-blown market economy!

Chapter 3 - Protest and Poaching

When I left school at 14, I got a job as a laundry van boy at 10 shillings a week, but I soon got the push. The van driver had taken a dislike to me for some reason I couldn't quite understand. He was a rather crude self-opinionated individual who liked to throw his weight around. I suppose it gave him a sense of power to be able to have me sacked.

Some time later I got a start at a wool merchants' where my elder brother worked. I have often speculated why Alec took on this job. He had been dux of the school. There is no doubt he is very intelligent, quite a different character from me. I had hoped he would become a writer. He could describe a commonplace incident in such an amusing way that it kept you giggling for hours afterwards. Alec was also very particular about his appearance. Ruthie called us the Devil and the Dandy. I was not the refined one. That Alec stayed on at that job until he was called up to the army indicates how difficult it was for a bright boy to get employment worthy of his talent.

At that time young people of our social standing never thought of having a career or even of getting a white-collar job. That was going above our station. For a boy, the highest ambition would be to become an apprentice in the building trade. For a girl, a shop assistant's job in the Co-op was something to boast about. I remember one boy in our street did sit an examination for a position as a counter clerk in the Post Office. This was looked on as something out of the ordinary and we talked about being in the Civil Service.

An enterprising Yorkshire man had started up this small wool merchant business. There was nothing else of its kind in the district. The job consisted of sorting out the different qualities of wool from the fleeces of different breeds of sheep. Some of the wool would be suitable for making tweeds and much of it went to the mills on the island of Lewis. The rough qualities were supposed to go to carpet makers, but the belief was that it found its way to Italy to be made into blankets for Mussolini's troops who were invading Abyssinia at the time. We often got letters from crofters on Scottish islands enclosing a couple of pounds for some wool for their hand looms. Apparently, the big mills tried to corner all the supplies of local wool and push the hand-loom weavers out of business.

Wool-sorting was supposed to be a trade and I was supposed to be an apprentice, but most of the work was labouring. Enormous sacks were strung from the rafters and the sorted wool was thrown in, then I got in and stamped and stamped till it was as solid as a rock. By the time I was 17, I was getting 17/6d for a 48-hour week. I was already an ardent socialist by this time. That was OK by the boss; we all worked together and talk was freely exchanged. He even urged me to graduate from reading Kier Hardie, to a study of Karl Marx. Hardie was a local miner in his day.

It so happened that just at that time the *Daily Herald* was running a series of articles about low pay in the wool trades and it appeared that one of the jobs I had to do was rated in Bradford at £2 a week. I refused to do the job and talked about forming a union. Of course, that was not very wise in a small shop with half a dozen employees, and so I was sacked on the spot.

Soon afterwards I got casual work in a scrap yard. The war machine was starting up. Iron was needed and there was plenty in the derelict pits and factories. My job was to break the large pieces of cast iron with a 28 lb hammer and pack it into empty oil drums for easier transportation to the furnaces. I hardly had the physique for such heavy work so I took up poaching in a more serious way.

Unfortunately, on one of these expeditions in the High Parks I was caught with a couple of rabbits in my possession. The solicitor acting for the Duke of Hamilton – Souttar by name – was an Elder in St John's Church of which my mother was a member. At one stage I had to appear before him. He proposed that if I signed a statement that I would not trespass on the High Parks again no further action would be taken against me. I refused to go along with this. I suppose that was a bit stupid, for I am sure Souttar was anxious to dispose of this rather petty business and avoid the embarrassment of court action against one he thought as a member of his congregation. But if I am not too conceited I think my action indicated even at that early stage in my life that I was beginning to take up a principled position even if it was at some personal cost. In the end, I did appear in court and was fined £5. That was a lot of money in those days and it worried me a great deal. My unemployment benefit was 14 shillings a week. There was never a penny left over from the family house-keeping expenses, but I knew my mother wouldn't let me go to jail through failure to pay the fine. I solved the problem by stepping up my poaching activities.

Most of my poaching was carried out in the High Parks, the Duke of Hamilton's estate. It wasn't cultivated very much, but was suitable for grazing. Incidentally, it contains the skeletons of oaks that were said to date back to Roman times and also a herd of rare sacrificial cattle. The value of the estate lay in the coal seams underneath which provided the

Hamilton family with the proceeds of mineral royalties. The Duke's son was supposed to be courting Lady Prunella Stack, the leader of the Woman's League of Health and Beauty, which we took as being modelled on a similar organisation in Nazi Germany. Interestingly enough, a few years later when Britain went to war with Hitler, Rudolph Hess his deputy, landed secretly by plane in a nearby estate of the Duke's. We have still to learn the inside story.

My regular poaching companion was Sammy Irvine, the most expert poacher I ever came across. He was considerably older than me – in his mid-30s – and was married with one child. He was one of that big segment of young men in Hamilton at that time who had no proper employment since leaving school. But Sammy earned a little bit on the side as a boxer in the second-rate boxing circuit in Lanarkshire. There was no question of training or medical examination. You just appeared in the ring and started slogging. I saw only one contest and found it so brutal that it was my first and last. Later, Sammy was caught poaching in the High Parks and got such a beating from gamekeeper and police that his involvement in the 'noble art' was over for good.

Poaching was never regarded by country people as a criminal activity; rather it was seen as the poor getting some of their own back of the heritage had been stolen from them by Dukes and Lairds. Although I think I had a fine sense of what was right and what was wrong I never felt any shame about my poaching activities. In any case, the balance was very much against us, especially in the High Parks. In my time the gamekeeper was called Bartleman. His brother was a sergeant in Hamilton police and the police had more or less free rein to shoot over the estate as the Hamilton family rarely visited it. There was something of a law of the jungle relationship between us poachers and the estate workers. It was very much a question of who got in the first blow.

Old Bob Hannah was the rabbit catcher. He used to set his snares on a Wednesday so as to be able to take his catch to the butcher on Thursday, the best selling day. We would creep quietly through the woods till we found which fields he was working. Then late that night we would lift the rabbits out of his snares – we called that double-poaching. A wet windy night was best for there was less chance of anyone being about. You might ask: was that fair? My reply is that more often the boot was on the other foot – sometimes even up your backside!

Quite often it was the poacher who lost his catch and all his equipment. If the keeper surprised you, you had to run for it and leave ferret, nets and everything else behind. If you were caught the best you could hope for was a beating. It happened to me. I was trapped by the son of one of the gatekeepers and some of his pals. They had their fun at my expense then let me go. Although I had a few bruises I greatly appreciated their action

19

in not handing me over to the police. Soon afterwards one of them joined the police force in Hamilton. When we met in the street I always gave him a polite nod. This was my way of saying 'thanks' for not having me put inside on that occasion.

Over the years I came to think of the High Parks and the Ross Estate as my territory, and even at times roamed around with my shotgun although that was not a favoured poacher's implement. For one thing it made too much noise and gave away your whereabouts. More important, even in those far off days a cartridge cost 2d, and anyway damaged the flesh of anything that had been shot. I paid two pounds and ten shillings for that gun, or at least for the pawn ticket from another poacher who had fallen on bad times.

Most of my poaching was done by ferreting. It was quieter. The only trouble was that sometimes the ferret would 'lie in'; that is kill the rabbit and stay down the burrow and go to sleep. In that event you had the laborious job of digging it out. I once thought of a quicker way. The carbide from a miner's lamp gives off an inflammable gas when in contact with water. I crawled into the burrow as far as I could go, laid some wet grass on the carbide and lit a match. The intention was to smoke the ferret out. There was an almighty explosion from the accumulated gas in the confined space. I was blinded – I thought for ever. Luckily my sight came back, but for some time I had no hair, eyebrows or eyelashes.

Another method of catching rabbits was with a long net. This had to be done on a dark stormy night when the rabbits were well out in the field where they would 'clap down' in the long grass. When the net was set you would circle behind them and drive them into the net. I had a dog – the most intelligent one I ever possessed – who worked the rabbits in the same way that a collie drives sheep into a pen.

I went through a few dogs in those days and came to realise that they had a range of 'personalities' very much like human beings. The one that I have just referred to had a morose disposition but he could anticipate what I wanted of him without me having to give the order. I had another one, a highly strung yuppie, who was so stupid that he would gobble down a bowl of sawdust if I put it down to him at feeding time. He was no use for my purposes.

On one occasion I had a lesson on human morality. Sixpence was the most you got for a rabbit from the butcher. But the greyhound owners proffered half a crown for a live one when they wanted to keen their dog for a race. As it so happened, one of my pals was a street bookie and a greyhound owner as well, and when the 'clique' planned to fix a race he would ask me to get him a live rabbit. Instead of giving me the half crown he would put it on the intended winner for me. He thought he was doing me a favour. But it never worked out. Greyhound racing on the unlicensed courses in those days was so crooked that even the crooks themselves were done.

For my bookie friend it was all part of the game. But for me? Since then I have never laid a penny on horses, dogs or sweepstakes. Is this because the rabbit business taught me a lesson about gambling or does it simply expose the character of a mean miserable Scotsman? The one thing I am certain of is that I have become a little bit more civilised and would not now provide a live rabbit for greyhound coursing.

In my old age I cannot escape from thinking about the morality question connected with poaching: was it thieving? Just think: a night's expedition would mean travelling through woods or over rough ground for four or five miles in the dark and often cold and wet weather. The heaviest bag would be eight or ten rabbits; that would be coming towards half a hundredweight on your back to carry home. And when you went to the butcher next day you would be lucky to get five shillings. Thieving? Something for nothing? No – it was hard bloody work!

I should say something about my parents. Of my mother's background I know very little. I never met a single relative and she never talked about anyone connected to her. I have her photograph as a young woman. She was quite striking in appearance. My father must have been middle-aged when he married her, not much more than a girl. Father had been a watchmaker then for some reason joined the regular army and served a long time in Africa. He didn't talk much about it but sometimes when we pestered him he would show us the dried skin of what once was a large boa constrictor snake with a three cornered hole pierced in it where he had killed it with his bayonet. What flights of imagination about jungle adventures I had when I saw it.

Father never returned to his trade and found work on the railway. While I was still a schoolboy, he retired at 70 years of age. Somehow he had falsified his age making out that he was five years younger. From then on his health deteriorated and in the last few years before he died he was bedridden.

I was very close to my father. I think the closest in the family. When I returned from an outing I would stand by his bedside and tell him about all the things I had seen; an otter, a fox, or some rare bird or animal. It was like both of us being on the expedition all over again. There was a touch of nostalgia in his voice when he said, "You always see much more than I did when I was your age."

When father died I felt completely broken. I've had other bereavements since but none that left me so completely empty.

My father's father died a long time before I came into the world, the stories we were told about him were very exciting. As a young man he had to flee from his Highland home when the Laird's men caught him poaching salmon. His was the classic case of poacher turned gamekeeper – or at least policeman – for he ended up as sergeant of police in Hamilton. With that background it made us quite a well-known and respectable family. Father had one brother and three sisters. The brother, our uncle John, had a joinery business in the Grangemouth shipyard. He was quite prosperous. He was very religious and rather self-important. I remember the one and only time he visited us. My mother scrubbed the place from end to end. She cut up an old bed sheet so that we would all have hankies. We had to put on our best clothes and were warned to be on our best behaviour. We were going to be short of chairs so Davie, our eldest brother, mended an old one with a piece of plywood and polished it till it was shining, the best looking chair in the house.

When Uncle John arrived we were all gathered round him to pay homage. He was a great big bulk of a man. Mother ushered him into Davies chair. There was an ominous crackling sound. The plywood seat was not stout enough to take his weight. He jumped up and the chair came along with him. His great fleshy buttock was caught firmly in the crack. It must have been terribly painful. What a disastrous outcome for mother after all the work she had put in to create a good impression. Uncle John said grace at the meal. I don't know what he told the Lord under his breath for we never heard a word from Uncle John after that.

Aunt Maggie was the only relative who lived in our town. She was married to a lawyer and had a posh house less than half a mile away. She must have felt superior and wanted to keep us at a distance for there never was an exchange of visits. One time when mother was at her wits end about money she decided to go to Aunt Maggie and ask for a loan. This was torture for mother. She had to force herself to do it. She took me with her for moral support. I think we came back empty handed for we were not even invited through the door.

Aunt Jean lived in Glasgow about 12 miles away. She sometimes visited us but when I was arrested and appeared in court for poaching she sent a letter to my mother saying I had brought shame and disgrace on the good name of the Nicolsons. My sister Ruth was indignant and dictated a stinging letter for mother to reply. Ruthie always stood by me right or wrong showing that there was more solidarity in our poor family than in father's family who had moved up in the world. But that was the end of Aunt Jean's visits.

Being poor and with no prospects of things getting better, mother had to invent an anodyne. It was that father being the oldest one in his family was the rightful heir to a farm that had belonged to some distant relative who was without descendants. It had gone elsewhere, but mother had us almost convinced that justice would triumph in the end and we would move from our overcrowded urban slum and go and live in rural splendour. It was our cocaine, a lovely dream.

Strangely, for the past couple of years when holidaying in Scotland I have passed by a farm of the name she gave. I was tempted to go in and find out something about it but felt too embarrassed to give the reason for my interest. I'm not sure if I can find the place again. If I do I will pluck up courage and satisfy my curiosity.

Chapter 4 - Politics and the Railway Yard

I have had some kind of socialist ideas from as early as I was able to think about life around me. My parents were Labour voters. However, I don't recall politics being discussed in the home. I've already mentioned the interest aroused by the missionaries' tales of poverty and disease in Africa. But I'm sure the weightiest factor was the poverty in our own community. I can remember as a child pondering long and hard over the question: why can't the cobbler get his bread from the baker and in return mend the baker's shoes with a similar kind of exchange between workers in various occupations? In a childish way I had stumbled on the idea of a barter system as the solution to humanity's unhappiness. I thought: when I grow up and preach this gospel people will see the light.

It was Maurice Shinwell, younger brother of the famous Manny, who put socialism in more practical terms for me even before I had become a teenager. He was running for a seat on Hamilton Council and used to hold meetings of the unemployed at the Low Quarry, which I had to pass on my way home from school. I was mesmerised. His message clicked immediately. I was always late home from school when he was around. The explanation that I was at a political meeting seemed a very lame excuse to my mother.

By the time I had left school I was attending Labour College classes and other political meetings. Hamilton at that time had quite a lot of political groups: Labour Party, Independent Labour Party (ILP), Socialist Party of Great Britain (SPGB), Communist Party, two different Anarchist groups, and followers of a weird knicker-bockered individual called Guy Aldred, who always had a harem of formidable women around him and published a paper called *The Word*. These groups were fiercely antagonistic towards each other. On a summer evening I have seen a dozen of them sat around on the grass going at it hammer and tongs, then someone could hold out no longer and pulled out a woodbine, and after a few puffs it had to be passed round the circle, the ones at the end having to hold it with a pin – the craving was stronger than the conflict!

The most feared debater was wee Wully Stewart of the SPGB. He would silence you with a quote from Karl Marx page so and so volume so and so. But Wully betrayed the cause in the end – or so we pretended to ourselves in revenge for all the wounds he had inflicted on us. He took a job as a time-keeper at the construction of the Scapa Flow submarine base. Not only was it a war job, it was a white-collar one where he didn't dirty his hands; he had moved over to the bourgeoisie! What a fate! Scapa Flow is the coldest, stormiest, most inhospitable place on the North Atlantic coast.

The Spanish Civil War and what was going on in Nazi Germany stirred political passion in Britain. I often travelled into Glasgow on Sunday nights where the Communist Party held big 'Aid Spain' meetings in West George Street. It was at one of these that I handed up my first big donation a 10 shilling note – a lot of money for me at that time. I must have been very much moved by the appeal.

I was gradually moving towards the Communist Party. There was a CP bookshop in Blantyre and a Party branch with some very fine mining comrades, and a very articulate Councillor, Eddie Laughlan. I used to go there and talk for hours on end, hoping that I would be asked to join the Party. But the comrades appeared to be very cagey about this. I learned later that it was because they were all ex-Catholics and equally keen to recruit someone from a Protestant background, but cautious about putting the question too soon in case it would frighten me off. In the end it was Bob Harvie, a miners' son and university graduate, not much older than myself, who joined me up.

Strange as it may seem, Bob Harvie played some part in the 50s in helping to launch Robert Maxwell's publishing empire. At that time universities were rapidly expanding and Maxwell started publishing student textbooks. Bob was employed to advise him on works that would have a good selling potential. Maxwell's business acumen came in by getting the books printed in East Germany (the German Democratic Republic or GDR) where that kind of printing technique was quite advanced; only the book covers were printed in Britain. This got round some kind of ban on trade with the GDR so the books could be exported to the US as well. I got to know all this because Bob used to travel from Oxford, where he was working with Maxwell, and spent the weekend with us in London until my wife Bridget got fed up with us sitting up till the early hours emptying the bottle of whisky that always accompanied Bob on these visits.

But back to Blantyre. We used to have public meetings on Sunday nights. The District office in Glasgow allocated the speaker. Our job was to chalk the streets advertising the meeting. On this occasion the name we got was Sam Aaronovitch. We had not heard of him before. So the following conversation took place between the other chalker and me: Joe: "Aaron... that means Jew." Me: "vitch... that means Russian." Thereupon the meeting was advertised thus: "COME AND HEAR SAM AARONOVITCH THE

RUSSIAN JEW" etc. It looks funny. But there is something significant in it as well. At that time there was much sympathy for the plight of the Jews in Nazi Germany, and any information about Russia was gobbled up. It also indicated the internationalist outlook characteristic of the movement in Scotland.

Soon after the beginning of the war I became secretary of the Hamilton branch. The membership consisted mainly of miners, rail workers, steel-workers and engineers who had moved by this time from the dole queue to munitions. The Party at that time was still very Puritanical. I remember being puzzled by a shadow that hung over one of the older members, Jimmy L, from Eddlewood. The wholesalers wouldn't handle the *Daily Worker* so there was a rota of members who walked all the way to Mother-well to catch the newspaper train when it came in before five in the morning and bring them back to Hamilton. One particularly blustery morning Jimmy was so frozen that he used a couple of coppers from the paper money for a cup of tea and a hot pie. This was regarded as improper and haunted Jimmy for a long time.

With Hamilton being a barracks town we made contact with members from other parts of the country who had been called up to the army. It was the Phoney War period and, in my youthful naiveté, I thought things might develop in the same way as the First World War, and we could be confronted with a revolutionary situation before long. For myself, there was an element of eager anticipation in this. So when there were jokes about smuggling arms out of the barracks it was something of a thrill for me. But as so very often happens, real life took a very different turn. It was around this time that I started work on the railway. I got a start as a 'caller up' at Hamilton West locomotive depot. It was a night shift job. I cycled through the town in the early hours of the morning and knocked up drivers and guards who were due on duty before 6am. In those days even the aristocrats of labour didn't have telephones. I had to make sure that they got up and booked on at the right time.

In the depressed 30s you had to be lucky to get a job on the railway. Pay wasn't good but the attitude was that it was a job for life, and that was an important consideration when it looked as if unemployment was going to be with us forever. My father had worked at the depot and my eldest brother Davie until his call up to the army, so I qualified to be put on the waiting list.

How Davie came to get his job there illustrates the pre-war labour situation. The 1926 General Strike had so alarmed the authorities that they decreed that each loco depot had to lay down thousands of tons of coal each year as a precaution against a similar emergency at some future date, with an equal quantity of the old stock being uplifted for current use. This was done by temporary labour during the summer months, and if you were so employed for three or four years you had a good chance of getting a regular job. It was backbreaking work for very little pay. That is what Davie had to go through to get a dirty, greasy, low paid job as a fitter's labourer, but on a regular basis.

There had been a panic call-up in the early stage of the war. But it turned into the Phoney War with few troops in action and the danger of a labour shortage in the less attractive industries. Many miners were actually demobilised and sent back to the pits. Soon railway recruitment stopped, so I remained a civilian rail worker all during the war. It also meant that my promotion to locomotive fireman was quite rapid.

There was little romance in being a fireman. It was dirty, hard, manual work. During a shift you would shovel several tons of coal into the firebox while you were doubled up and twisting round every few seconds while standing on a moving floor so that you staggered like a drunken man when you stepped off the engine. In winter, snot would be dropping from your nose with cold while your backside was being roasted. It could be dreary; up and down, up and down for hours on end in the shunting yard. You worked round the clock. Only those who have done it know what it is to be asleep and awake at the same time. I've had two minutes of shovelling alternating with two minutes of the soundest sleep imaginable while the driver had his head over the other side of the cab on the lookout for signals.

The depot produced a remarkably large number of interesting characters. Perhaps this was because at that time television did not exist. Each person had to do his own thinking; he was his own man, three dimensional, not a stereotype. It was the people I worked with who made life interesting, not the job itself. I'm thinking of one of my drivers, old Joe Moore. He was a poet of some accomplishment. His poems appeared regularly in the *Blantyre Gazette*! As a workmate Joe was rather on the surly side, rarely speaking. He seemed to be making up rhymes in his head all the time; that was good enough company for him. Physically, Joe was a great bear of a man. It was rumoured that if he fell out with another driver he would piss on his engine firebox – and wouldn't that leave some stink! No one ever challenged Joe about this.

Old Willie Wilson the atheist was such a different character. He was very gentle, didn't smoke, drink or use foul language. It was a great relief for an inexperienced fireman when he was put on with Willie. He knew he would not be humiliated if he failed to keep up steam. Willie would coach you in such a kindly way that made you feel that it was you who were doing him a good turn rather the other way round. He was a friend of our family and used to pass on his rationalist magazine to my father. When father was nearing his end and started reading spiritualist literature, Willie became very sad.

Then there was Bob Reid 'the rancher'. He lived in an isolated railway cottage about a mile away from the depot where he kept a mini-zoo. He was always dressed in the same dirty old oily dungarees, on duty or off. You would come across him collecting dandelion leaves or thistle seeds for his 'little creatures'. This is what he lived for. His job as engine driver was a kind of sideline to enable him to provide for them.

At the beginning of the war there was uncertainty about what was happening. People had expected to be blasted by bombs, perhaps suffer poison gas attacks – gas masks had been issued – or that spies or invaders would drop from the sky. Nothing happened. Everyone was jumpy. I came off work early one morning and took my dog for a walk along the left bank of the Avon. I sat down under a tree and took a paper out of my pocket. There was a whistle from the opposite bank where a couple of policemen must have been watching me all the time. They wanted to know what I was up to. They were not satisfied with my answer. They were suspicious. There were plenty of works of military importance around. The sergeant ordered the constable to cross the river though it was waist deep. I was taken to the Ross House and held there till my identity was confirmed. Later, when escorted by the police down the drive, trotting alongside us was my little dog with a rabbit in her mouth.

In our area we didn't experience any bombing throughout the war. At one stage German bombers did pass over us night after night to bomb Clydebank about 20 miles away. Only once did a stray bomb fall near us. It landed on a soft cinder embankment about a couple of hundred yards from our house. No one was injured, though wagon fragments tore through the roof of the council tenement in White Hill Road.

I suppose the monotony of our diet was the biggest grouse, though most people had more nutritious food than they had known before. With more money around there was a lot of drinking on Saturday nights and pubs were foggy with cigarette smoke.

Women also were now working in munitions factories. A trainload of them used to leave Hamilton every morning at 5am for Bishopton, where explosives were made. It was unhealthy work. The women had sallow complexions through long hours in toxic fumes. Old-fashioned attitudes still lingered. Women who worked in these big factories were thought of as being of coarse and of dubious morals. More than once the superintendent at Hamilton allowed an engine to be used that could not heat their carriages. That would never have been allowed for ordinary passengers.

After the Soviet Union came into the war on June 22nd 1941 political attitudes began to change. Up till then there had been a feeling of doom. The Nazis seemed invincible on the battlefield. France and the rest of

Europe had collapsed. There had been plenty of collaborators among the ruling families. Would the same thing happen in Britain? The feeling of ordinary people was one of uncertainty and political distrust.

The resistance of the Soviet people and their leaders to the massive offensive of the Germans was so different from what had happened so far in the war with their scorched earth policy and mass human heroism on a scale surpassing anything known in history. How was it that the Soviet people were capable of such bravery? All the horror stories about Soviet communism were beginning to be questioned. There was a widespread desire to get to know more about socialism.

Now it was much easier for communists to work openly. We were swimming with the stream. People wanted to show their support for the Soviet Union. The sales of communist literature round the pubs and housing schemes grew rapidly. I remember Bernard Shaw wrote a pamphlet *Shaw on Stalin*. We sold the entire issue on one Saturday night and could have sold thousands more. Paper was rationed and we were always agitating for a bigger allocation.

One of the things I marvel at when I think back is just how much energy we must have had. We worked hard at our job, in fact we all tried to be model workers, as an example to the others, performing our duties efficiently and saving fuel and other material. Sometimes this involved working overtime. Then, after work there was always some political business to do. Weeknights it would be branch meetings or Marxist classes to attend. Saturday evening was for *Worker* sales round the pubs, and on Sunday mornings we did the housing rounds. We had a blind comrade, Martin Milligan, who sold five dozen papers door to door every Sunday.

Early in the war I was already addressing public meetings. As our main demand was for the Second Front, it is not surprising that I should be asked why I was not in the Forces. Actually I had volunteered twice, if I remember correctly, by letter. I didn't push it further than that. There was a small group of anarchist miners who regularly threw this at me. I challenged them to do something about it. They were rather foolish to pick up the bait. Two of them who lived near me escorted me to Guy Aldred their anarchist guru. He dismissed them, but John McGovern, an ILP MP and rabid anti-communist took it up with the War Department. Ultimately, a reply came back that I was in a reserved occupation and would be dealt with in the same way as others in that category.

More serious opposition to the war came from a Trotskyite group led by Gibbie Russell, who came from a well known and respected local mining family. He edited *The Scottish Militant Miner* and tried to build up support with sales at pit-heads. Fortunately Communist influence in the pits was sufficient to nullify this effort. Still, with miners beginning to regain their confidence after the shabby way they had been treated between the wars and there was always a danger of a spark starting a conflagration.

Later the anarchists organised a visit by the Duke of Bedford, a pacifist opponent of the war, to the Lanarkshire coalfield. We had our revenge. The area was plastered with the slogan: 'Keep the Fascist Duke Out', no doubt an over-reaction, but typical of our partisan attitude at that time.

It was at this time that I first met Dan Kelly. He was a wagon examiner at Shieldhall Docks. I attended a lecture he gave on dialectical materialism. This is a difficult philosophical concept about change. It was used to explain the Communist Party's switch from opposition to support for the war. I was immensely impressed that a working man like myself could master such complex ideas. I retained a deep respect for Dan's ability when years later he served on the NUR's executive.

Another leading communist I came in contact with was Jock Shearer. He was a signalman at West Street Junction, just outside Glasgow. He became a much respected divisional officer in the union. I often spent hours with him in the signal box. This was because our mineral train was often held up at the junction to allow American troop trains to pass through. American convoys came into Greenock and it would need many trains to move the tens of thousands of soldiers who disembarked there.

When the Americans went past a populated place they would throw out packets of cigarettes till the line side was covered with them. We picked them up for popular brands were often scarce in the shops. But we had mixed feelings about this; we were a proud people, not paupers.

We weren't always so morally upright. The American convoys did not return empty. They took back Scotch whisky. One night-shift we worked a train into Greenock yard. There had been a rough shunt earlier and a vat had been damaged with the whisky slowly dribbling on to the ground. The excise officers were there to see that every drop soaked into the cinders. A few disgruntled railwaymen, infuriated at such senseless waste, hung around in the shadows. I don't know how it was done but the excise men were decoyed away. Every pot and pan in the place was mobilised to salvage the precious liquid. We were happy. Part of our national heritage had been saved!

Only a few months before the time of writing, something similar happened. This time it was a container consigned to Japan that was the casualty. It appears that the Japanese have bought up many of our Scottish distilleries. I suppose we should welcome this inward investment. I just hope it doesn't mean that too much of what is good in our country flows outwards. I certainly enjoyed that stuff even though it was presented to me in a giant lemonade bottle.

Chapter 5 - Council candidate and Lanarkshire Secretary

In 1943 there was a by-election in Hamilton. Duncan Graham, a miners' MP, who had held the seat since 1918, died. The miners regarded it as their seat. But there was a right-wing conspiracy to get Ian Dean, a Hamilton councillor and Scottish organiser of the Labour Party, adopted. The miners were in some difficulty for most of their prominent members were communists. In the end they chose Tom Fraser, a totally unknown young pit delegate in a small colliery near Lesmahagow. I think I can say in all truth that it was my effort in the Hamilton Branch of the NUR that swung the vote in his favour. This was enough to give him a bare majority at the Labour selection conference. The main parties held to the electoral truce that had been agreed for the duration of the war. But Fraser was challenged by Johnnie Letham, an engine driver at the Kipps depot in Coatbridge, who stood as an Independent. Fraser won. The largest meeting he addressed as a new MP was one I organised for medical aid for Russia.

Fraser was made Minister of Transport in the 1964 Wilson Government. He failed to implement Labour's manifesto pledge to halt the Beeching cuts to the railway. This provoked a revolt of NUR MPs and Wilson was forced to sack Fraser. According to Professor Bagwell, the North London District Council of the NUR played a significant role in this. The District Council was my stamping ground at the time. I became its secretary shortly afterwards.

Towards the end of the war the main parties started to prepare for a general election. As part of this the NUR launched a campaign to get union members to 'contract in' to the political fund of the union, which is used to finance the Labour Party. Making contact with rail workers who book on at different locations and at individual times round the clock was quite a formidable task. Although I was a communist and not in the Labour Party, I played a big part in this campaign. Our NUR branch had done so well that we got a special commendation from our head office.

The 1945 election was a really exhilarating experience. As the servicemen's votes had to be collected from all over the globe it meant that each constituency result was announced separately over a period of many days. There was no doubt about our constituency. It was rock solid Labour. But whenever a result came over the radio total strangers would gather in groups in the street and excitedly tot up the score.

Later that year I stood as the communist candidate in the council elections in Hamilton and polled a creditable vote. Recently I came across a pamphlet I wrote for that campaign 'HAMILTON – A TOWN WITH A FUTURE?' After all those years I feel mildly impressed by that contribution at such a young age.

I am looking at a Broadsheet that we published for that election. We sold well over a thousand copies in the Ward. Here are a very few extracts:

ON JOBS:
In the Douglas Valley coalfield there are big possibilities of development and in the normal course of events much of this coal will be transported via rail yards in the neighbourhood of Hamilton. Surely it is reasonable to suggest that preparations be made for the erection of a plant in Hamilton for the extraction of chemicals, dye stuffs, synthetic oil, plastics, and the many other possible derivatives of coal...

ON HOUSING:
Are we therefore driven to the conclusion that there are families who must wait until 1956 or later for a home of their own. The Communist Party does not accept this conclusion. We say the job can be done in half the time – but only if in addition to speeding up orthodox building, we introduce on a large scale new building methods... we need go no further than Glenlee Street or Robertson Street in Burnbank – the residence of the better-paid sections of the workers – to see how substantial and pleasant a prefabricated house can be. There you have the 'Atholl' type of steel prefabricated house still standing after twenty years, still attractive to look at and comfortable to live in...

ON EDUCATION:
The shift of part of Hamilton's population to Fairhill and Udston housing schemes makes it imperative that the first of the new schools should be erected in this area.

ON LOCAL GOVERNMENT FINANCE:
We are therefore fighting to win the support of the Labour movement and the Local Authorities for the setting up of a Government Commission which would be charged with the job of working out the details of a practicable and reasonable system of local income tax.

Later that year we published a weightier pamphlet entitled 'Hamilton Fights for the Future'. By this time we were able to say...

"The demand for a coal distillation plant in Lanarkshire first proposed by the Communist Party, is now being pressed by the Lanarkshire trades councils, and is likely to bear fruit. Coal distillation would provide the basis of a whole number of ancillary industries employing a large number of people... Steel, with coal is the flesh and bone of our economy..."

"...There has been a welcome development of light industries in the area in recent years... But all these factories will employ mainly female labour. One inescapable fact emerges from all this: mid-Lanarkshire must have an alternative basic industry for the progressive employment of male labour..."

Then there is the stirring peroration of the pamphlet:

"Hamilton has a past. Much of it is sordid and miserable; the filching of the common lands by luxury living aristocrats; the coal owners shameless exploitation of the miners; the slum landlords' blatant disregard of all human decencies. But there is another prouder side to the picture. It was the excessive suffering that placed Hamilton in the forefront of marching humanity from the days of Chartism, right through the mining struggles to become the birthplace of Kier Hardy, the cradle of the Socialist Movement. And because Hamilton, perhaps more than any other town, represents the problems of the future, the emergence of the Communist Party, the most modern expression of the progressive strivings of humanity – is an event of the greatest significance."

Perhaps a bit florid, even romantic. But it does show that we were close to the problems of ordinary people and had an overall, but practical view of what should be done. Another thing is our pride in our own people's history and our attempt to bring that spirit to life. I think that distinguished us from the more pedestrian pragmatism of the Labour Party at that time.

A very sad event occurred not long after that election. Archie Lang who had been my election agent was killed in a motorbike accident. Archie's father, Guy Lang, was a staunch atheist-socialist of the older generation. He had been one of John McLean's followers in pre-First World War days and had been responsible for organising McLean's Marxist economic classes in Burnbank. Interestingly, all these old socialists understood Marx's theory of surplus value; for them it was the absolute basic of socialist understanding. Anyway Guy asked me to do the funeral oration. I was hesitant. I felt too young and inexperienced, and had never done anything like it before. Besides, I was emotionally involved in the death of a comrade I had worked with so closely only recently. But Guy insisted.

The Lang family were closely-knit on all sides. But Guy and his side were atheists whereas Archie's wife still held vaguely religious beliefs. She was shattered by the death. Her position had to be respected. So here we were at the family service in her home: a reverend on one side of the corpse delivering a religious service, and I following on the other side with an atheist and socialist tribute. At the cemetery there was a public service, and as it was not the custom for women to be at the graveside, I did it on my own. There was quite a gathering of Labour notables present for the Lang family were well-known and highly respected. I, young and inexperienced, let my tongue run away with itself about the touchstone of socialist purity being recognition of the Soviet Union as the fatherland of all workers. This upset many Labour Party members who were there.

We were immensely proud of Lanarkshire's militant tradition. The first experiment anywhere in the world to establish a communist community was Robert Owen's New Lanark Colony. This was a protest against the harsh conditions of the early factory system and an attempt to humanise working and living conditions of the new industrial working class.

By the middle of the last century Lanarkshire was the centre of much of heavy industry in Scotland: coal and iron mining, iron and steel works, and railways. By the end of the century there were around 60,000 miners and something like 200 pits scattered throughout the county and big iron and steel works in Motherwell, Cambuslang, Airdrie and Coatbridge. By this time trade unions and labour organisations were firmly established. Lanarkshire produced Alexander McDonald, the first national leader of the miners' unions, and Kier Hardie, another Lanarkshire miner, became the first independent workers' leader to enter the British Parliament. The tradition continued when Walton Newbold, the first Communist Party member to become an MP was elected by Motherwell.

Between the two World Wars the Communist Party had become established in most of the towns and in many villages in Lanarkshire. In some of these we had town, county or parish Councillors. We also had members holding branch and district positions in all the important unions. Communists had been particularly active in the 1926 General Strike. The daring deeds of some of them had already become part of the folklore of the working class movement. Communists had been the inspirers and backbone of the Unemployed Workers' Movement, a high profile organisation that won wide support among the poorest section of the community. The Party had also been the driving force of the Aid Spain Movement and in recruiting for the International Brigade.

Comparing all that with the rather pedestrian activities of the Labour Party it is not surprising that communists had a feeling of superiority; an attitude that though they were still a minority they were something of an elite within the Labour Movement. Then during the Second World War, especially after the Soviet Union came in on June 22nd 1941, the membership and influence of the Party began to grow. I've already talked about some of our activities in Hamilton during that period. In addition to being Branch Secretary I had become one of the leading activists in the Lanarkshire Area Committee of the Party. Then, in 1947 I was appointed Secretary/Organiser in Lanarkshire.

Looking back I am amazed at my audacity in taking on that responsibility. My main qualification must have been youthfulness and drive. The older generation of Party members were outstanding personalities of the Red Clyde days. The person I took over from, Peter Cregan was a particularly knowledgeable and intelligent individual who had moved up to the Scottish office of the Party. He was what we called a 'Red Professor': that is a person who had a period of training in the Comintern School in the Soviet Union. My own contemporaries in Lanarkshire were already showing their mettle as future leaders of the Working Class Movement. I'm thinking of Bob Henderson, Jimmie Sneddon, Mick McGahey, Frank Waters and a number of others.

My appointment as Lanarkshire Secretary was by the process that could be described as consensus. Both the Scottish and Lanarkshire leaderships were involved. Bob Henderson could have done the job but he was National Vice-President of his union and there was no question of taking him out of that position. Jimmie Sneddon could have been considered but he was in a leading position in Colville's steel works, the biggest establishment of its kind in Scotland. Besides, he had a young family and could not have survived on a Party wage, which was less than £5 a week at that time. In the end I was the unanimous choice and throughout my tenure I had the full support of the whole membership.

I had overall responsibility for every aspect of Party organisation and activity in Lanarkshire. I had one full-time assistant, sometimes two, who did the typing, duplicating, and kept control of the finances. My duties included keeping something like 15 town and village branches up to scratch. This meant seeing that branch meetings were held, members visited, their dues and donations collected, and that they were actively involved in all the issues that the Party initiated. We paid a lot of attention to Party education and succeeded in getting most branches to run classes. Sometimes I took the classes myself; that required quite a lot of preparation. We also held regular meetings of our comrades in all the main industrial establishments and unions, and from time to time produced leaflets and broadsheets on such issues as wages and closures.

By the time I had taken over in Lanarkshire the Cold War against communism, internationally and in Britain, was well under way. Ernest Bevin was Foreign Secretary and no Tory could have been more bellicose against Russia than he was. Sir Stafford Cripps, the Chancellor, had announced a programme of retrenchment and a wage freeze. The top right-wing trade union leaders, especially Will Lawthers of the Miners and

Deakin of the TGWU, called on workers to combat the communist influence in the unions. One of the jokes going round at that time was that Deakin had caught so many 'reds under the bed' that he had contracted scarlet fever. But many Labour MPs and union leaders refused to go along with red-baiting. Still, it was obvious that we were in for a period of very hard battles ahead.

Our general strategy at that time was to try and rouse the workers into pushing the unions and the Government towards a more left-wing policy. I have before me a folder we used to advertise a big rally in Hamilton Town Hall on Sunday February 1st 1948. Willie Gallacher our Communist MP was the main speaker.

We bussed people in from every town and village in Lanarkshire. The hall was packed to the ceiling. Here are the main points in the folder:

PEACE:
Break with the American warmongers.
FOOD:
Plan production. Expand trade with Russia, Eastern Europe and the Dominions.
HOUSES:
Cut the army, NOT the building labour force.
WAGES:
Slash profits. Cut prices. Raise wages.

One of my jobs was to arrange the speakers for the public meetings our branches held at weekends. In the summer there would be anything from half a dozen to a dozen meetings, some in halls and others at recognised open-air sites. Mick McGahey, later National Vice-President of the NUM, was just starting his speaking career at that time. Invariably, Mick got the time or the place mixed up. He would turn up at the wrong village, or if he succeeded in getting to the right place he would arrive in the evening for what should have been an afternoon meeting. It was never possible to be angry with Mick. He was always so genuinely full of remorse for his mistake. Our paths have crossed many times since then. I have followed Mick's union career right up to his retirement. I've often watched with admiration his skill in defusing a tense and potentially explosive situation at a packed conference with a combination of tact and firmness. A journalist once described Mick as 'old granite face." Yes, he had a lot of granite in his make up, but I have never met a more humane and charming individual. I am immensely proud that he was one of us.

Another of our mining contemporaries of those days was Frank Watters. Frank and his two brothers were at the heart of the miners' struggles in the Shotts area. Frank was the youngest and was our branch secretary. One by one the pits in the area were closed and Frank moved to Yorkshire where he became a Communist Party organiser in that coalfield. It was from Frank that young Arthur Scargill, who had just joined the Young Communist League, got his early training in militant coalfield politics. I don't think Frank was pleased when many years later we became critical of some of Arthur's tactics during the 1984 miners' strike.

It is very difficult for me not to keep on reminiscing about our mining comrades. Once my mind starts turning in that direction one after another appears before me. But I will confine myself to mentioning only one more miner. Actually, he was retired when I got to know him. He was the father of Bob Tennant our Douglas Water party branch secretary. He was still a fine figure of a man, quietly spoken and widely read. I always liked to visit Douglas Water. It was so remote and on the edge of a vast moor. And Bob's old man pointed out the place on that moor where some miners had hidden and looked after some pacifist of the First World War who had refused to be conscripted into the army.

Now to return to my duties as Lanarkshire party organiser. Another form of propaganda was the factory-gate meeting. They took place during the mid-day break. I or one of our local speakers would usually take these meetings. But occasionally we would be allocated some well-known personality. I remember this once caused some eyebrow raising from our audience. This meeting was held outside Redpath Brown's engineering factory near Cambuslang. Bob Henderson worked there at the time. He was highly respected by the workers and when Bob issued a leaflet about the meeting there was a full turn out at the gate. The speaker was Barbara Niven. Everyone knew the name for Barbara had a front page column in the *Daily Worker* every day. It was the financial appeal column. Now, here she was in the flesh. Slim and elegant in appearance and with a refined contralto voice she was up there on that platform calling on these rough tough industrial proletarians to roll up their sleeves and fight back to defeat the wage freeze. Somehow it didn't seem to fit.

A different kind of meeting – and it makes me smile when I think about it – was in connection with the Council elections in Motherwell. Two young men came into our office in Motherwell saying they were interested in the Party. The following evening I took them along to one of our meetings in the Town Hall. It was on the eve of the Borough Council elections. There was a little fellow, lean, sharp faced, thinning hair, but with an exceptionally powerful voice prancing up and down the platform: "Who wiz it that goat the prefabs built doon the glen? It wiz Wully Smith. Who wiz it that goat the rent increases stopped? It wiz Wully Smith. Who wiz it that goat the pay increases fur the markers in the Bridge Works? It wiz Wully Smith!"

The speech went on like that and always it was the same answer. "It wiz Wully Smith." Then one of the young men turned round to me and asked in a very wondering voice "Who is this Wully Smith?" I had to tell him "That's him that is speaking." These young men were very impressed and joined the Party that night and for many years afterwards were among our best activists.

Wully Smith was no bluffer. He might have been small and unimposing in appearance but he was a bundle of electricity, as quick and courageous as a tiger. He was shop stewards convenor at Motherwell Bridgeworks where both workers and management held him in some awe, but for totally opposite reasons.

By this time we were very critical of the Labour Government's domestic and foreign policy and most of our propaganda was about this. But I want to mention two rather different kind of issue that we took up to illustrate our internationalism, which was one of our strong characteristics. French miners had been on strike and the situation turned very nasty when the gendarmes opened fire and killed some of the miners. We organised collections in the pits and mining villages. One of our members, a house-wife, collected on her own over £50 door to door and from her neighbours. That was lot of money then. The other campaign was for the release of Tony Ambatielos, a Greek seamen's leader who had been im-prisoned by the Greek right-wing Government for his union and political activities. We organised a series of union branch meetings addressed by his Welsh-born wife Betty. In the end this campaign brought about his release. Years later I had the pleasure of working with both of them and other Greek activists in their community in Camden Town.

Steel was our second major industry. We organised seminars of our lead-ing people in Dalziel Steelworks, Clyde Ironworks and the various Coatbridge plants. Ours was the least damaged industry in Europe and we thought of it as becoming the major steel producer. We published broadsheets and leaflets to arouse interest among the steelworkers about the future. Below is an extract from one of these broadsheets I was re-sponsible for in 1948. By this time the Cold War was under way and we saw the Marshall Plan as being directed not only against the Soviet Union but also damaging to our own economy, and especially to our steel indus-try. It will also be noted that political conflict here in Britain, as well as on a world scale, had become much sharper.

"Steel is a key commodity under the Marshall Plan. The Marshall Plan is a war plan. And as armaments are very profitable, Wall Street wants a monopoly in steel production. They are pouring money into German heavy industry. They are rehabilitating Germany as an arms centre..." "Stunning"

"In Britain the steel shortage is the greatest single industrial handicap. It means big cuts in reconstruction, machinery, shipbuilding, schools, houses and on exports. To produce 14 million tons requires 8.4 million tons of scrap. From home industry we get 3.9 million tons, the balance to be found from outside sources is therefore 4.5 million tons..."

"Does American big business want to help? Of course not. For instance, a US Government mission has reported that 10 million tons of scrap are available in Western Germany. It recommends that vigorous efforts be made by the Military Government to obtain the major portion of this hoard..."

"Fifteen nations, with Britain, at the Paris Conference requested 1.4 million tons of steel scrap in 1948, rising to 2.2 in 1952..."

"Not an ounce said the Marshall Planners. On the other hand, finished steel exports from the U.S. are to be 2 1/2 times more than requested..."

Wherever we had members or influence it was fashionable to try and work out plans for economic expansion. 'Diversification' was one of our buzz words. We recognised the danger of relying only on the old heavy industries and wanted our share of new factories. John Gollan's *Scottish Prospects* published in 1948 is a very comprehensive programme for restructuring Scottish industry, agriculture and fisheries.

In the trades councils we threw our weight behind the Education Act and the Beveridge Report. Towards the end of the war we had been in favour of some kind of national government, including progressive Tories, Liberal and Labour representatives. That kind of broad popular government of all the anti-Nazi resistance forces was coming into power in all the liberated areas in Eastern Europe and we were thinking along similar lines for Britain. It was the Labour Party and the Tories who took up the narrower position of one party rule. I mention all this because the 'mindless militant' image that has been tagged on to the Communist Party is not quite accurate. It was the Cold War, internationally and at home, that pushed us into positions of confrontation and set the pattern for the next 45 years. I will make some comments on this later. Meantime back to more personal affairs.

In recent days there has been much beating of breasts at the revelation that the Communist Party received money from Moscow a long time ago. I won't comment on that now though a sense of balance won't go wrong. What I can say is that none of it ever came our way. What is more, full-timers in the Party received less pay than a manual worker and put in double the hours. I hope it does not look too pious to call this dedication and self-sacrifice.

Practically all the money we needed in Lanarkshire was raised from football sweeps in the pits and factories and from donations. Another important money-raiser was the Xmas bazaar. I remember having a narrow shave on an 'illegal' expedition to get material for our bazaar. I got the offer of a couple of hundredweight (cwt.) bags of sugar – it was rationed then – via a comrade who worked in a certain establishment. We waited till the place was empty on a Saturday afternoon. We needed to cross a field to get into the building unseen. On our return with the booty the car sank up to the axle in soft mud just as a policeman appeared round the corner. By an act of God – it couldn't have been anything else in that old crock – we pulled free as he approached us. The cake and candy stall was a great success that year!

You will see that I'm not claiming that as individuals we were pure. If what we had done had become known by any Party organisation we would have been seriously reprimanded at the very least. The Party's name must not be besmirched in the eyes of working people. That was the code of behaviour that was expected of us – and was generally observed. Yet, what we had done was not for self. I've not known anyone who enriched themselves through membership of the Communist Party.

Many people think that the Communist Party was only concerned with stirring up industrial unrest. That is a one-sided picture. In Lanarkshire much of our campaigning was about economic expansion. There was continuity in this. During the war our miners had been very much involved in pit production committees. It was the same in the steel works and other factories where we had influence. Often though, our lads were doing too much of the pushing and getting the back-wash from unpopular schemes. When the mines were nationalised in 1945 we continued to give production a high profile. Some of our activists became labour relations officers – in some cases, no doubt motivated by a desire for a softer job – but we would not have condoned that if we had not been anxious to see a revival of mining.

The past oppressed us. What was dominant in our mind was the need to avoid a return to mass unemployment. Lanarkshire is studded with monuments of the past: derelict pit heaps and abandoned collieries. There is a class element in this. To get quick profits the coal owners extracted the thick upper seams and allowed what was underneath to be flooded. That is market economics. A frightening thought: is the same thing happening with Scottish oil?

One of the ideas we plugged was for the underground gasification of coal. It wasn't a runner. The Labour Government was desperate for quick results. They opted instead for open-cast mining. I can't help thinking about what is happening to the coal industry today. It is vandalism. But what about all you people concerned to preserve the environment? It is all right using public money to safeguard what is on the surface? Why not the same reverence for nature's treasure that still lies underground?

Chapter 6 - With Willie Gallacher in West Fife

In 1947 I attended a course at the Party's residential school near Hastings and there met Bridget; that was the start of our life-long relationship. Bridget already had two children so could not leave London. I was hoping to move there to be with her. Instead, the Scottish Committee decided to send Murdoch Taylor, national secretary of the Young Communist League, and me to Fife. I accepted. There was a strong sense of Party discipline at that time. I felt obliged to go even though it conflicted with my own inclinations.

The reason for the move to Fife was that it was becoming clear that the Cold War was having such an effect that there was a danger of Willie Gallacher losing his Parliamentary seat. Gallacher was not only the best-known Communist in Britain, he was an international figure. He had been one of the most prominent leaders of the mass struggles of workers and tenants in Scotland during and after the First World War. Lenin had written Gallacher a sharp critique of the political errors of the Clyde leadership. This was made into a pamphlet *Left-Wing Communism – An Infantile Disorder* and became one of the world's best-known Marxist classics.

Gallacher already had a long association with West Fife before he became the MP in 1935. He became an effective parliamentarian and got plenty of publicity. He visited his constituency often and met many people. He did a lot of case work. To help with this he had a very conscientious full-time agent in the constituency. Besides, as an individual, Gallacher was warm-hearted and likeable. There were literally thousands of people who not only respected him as a politician, but also felt a deep personal affection for him. Even so the seat was in danger.

My first impression of the Party in Fife was not a very favourable one. There had been no full-time organiser for some time and things had become very slack. John Fernie was Gallacher's Agent in the constituency but his duties were mainly to handle case-work for Gallacher. Old Bob Selkirk and Mary Docherty manned the Fife Party office in Cowdenbeath but Bob was a pensioner and also a councillor so it was limited what they could do. What was needed in this sprawling constituency of West Fife were young, active organisers; that's why Murdoch Taylor and I had been sent there. Murdoch travelled back to his home in Edinburgh each night. I had lodgings in the same village as John Fernie; actually in the house of a very kind old aunt of his. Being in this position I did most of the running about to the farthest corners of the constituency, and was out from 9 o'clock in the morning until late at nights on week-ends as well.

My first discoveries were not very encouraging. Only 500 members had been registered, compared with 700 the previous year. And there was no money in the coffers. Worse, in common with most Party areas in Scotland one of our main money raisers was a Grand National Prize Draw, and here we were just a few weeks away from the race with only £26 having been handed in against prize money of £150. For me it was a frantic race from the first minute I landed in Fife.

The first branch meeting I attended was in the village of Bowhill. There were supposed to be 60 members in the branch but only 14 were in attendance. When I got there they were making a great mountain of a problem out of how to sell 13 *Soviet Weeklies*. I was outraged and kicked up hell with them. I had not intended to throw my weight about so soon; much better to wait till I knew the place better and the comrades knew me. However, my anger got results and before the meeting had finished I had four volunteers to take 11 dozen *Daily Workers* to the pit each Friday pay-day.

The *Daily Worker* was our main campaigning weapon. Within a few weeks pit-head sales had been extended to most of the pits where we had members. We also had door to door sales in many of the villages. On special occasions we would put on extras. For example when John Wood, who was Vice-President of the Scottish Area of the NUM, resigned from the Labour Party and applied to join the Communist Party we sold an additional 850 copies of the edition carrying that story. John Fernie and I sold 250 of them in Kelty where Wood resided. Incidentally, not long afterwards I personally recruited Leslie Wood, John's younger brother who had also been a Labour Party member.

Collecting for the Gallacher election fund was another regular pit-head activity. You simply stood outside the pay office and waved a collecting tin with a placard in the other hand saying what it was for. I took some of these collections myself when we couldn't cover a pit with locals and would raise from £6 to £8. I considered that quite good for someone not known by the miners. I have absolutely no hesitation in saying that we took every initiative that could be humanly expected of us to advance Gallacher's cause. He made a speech in Parliament in the devaluation debate. Straight away we had it printed and distributed it to all the branches in this scattered constituency. Within the next couple of days 3,000 had been sold at 1d each.

Another example of a rather different kind was a Gallacher Reception. This was aimed at broadening our base of non-Party contacts in the trade unions and strengthening our network of support groups for the election. It involved quite a lot of work in visiting our own members to help in compiling this list of potential supporters. But it was worth it. We got over 100 people to the Reception, each paying 4/6d for the honour of being invited to meet Gallacher, then contributing generously to the collection for the pleasure of the social evening. More important, quite a number of these non-Party people worked for Gallacher when the election came.

Naturally, most of my time and energy was taken up in organising the usual kind of activities of the Party. One of these was week-end propaganda meetings. Village halls had to be booked, speakers arranged and leaflets printed and distributed. Gallacher came into the constituency most week-ends. We were allocated national speakers such as Arthur Horner, but our own local speakers addressed most of the meetings. One of these that I have a record of was in the small mining and fishing village of Buckhaven. Jock McArthur, a popular Fife miners' leader who had just returned from a World Peace Congress was the speaker. 250 people turned up. It must have been one of the biggest assemblies the village had ever known. It was also a signal; the questions showered on him reflected the growing anxiety in ordinary people's minds about the direction communism was taking all over the world. They were about the Chinese shelling of a British warship on the Yangtze River, Russian policy of dividing Germany, and about the unrest communists were responsible for in many countries. I am not sure that I personally drew the correct conclusions from this event, for immediately afterwards I arranged and took a series of classes for Party members in that little village based on Stalin's book *The History of the CPSU(B)*.

A bit later I had a nasty experience of just how deep Cold War propaganda had bitten. I had arranged a public meeting for Gallacher in Valleyfield, which previously had been one of his strongholds. While distributing the leaflets advertising the meeting, one woman rushed back inside her house, set a match to the leaflets then threw it alight at me. "That's what I would do to all of you," she screamed. Only 20 people turned up to that meeting. It was unbelievable.

Previously Gallacher always had good attendances. There were about a dozen men hanging about just outside the hall and when I went out and tried to coax them into the meeting they told me: "We have nothing against Gallacher. He is a great man, but we hate his policies."

The Catholic Church in Fife was deeply involved in whipping up feeling against Gallacher. Priests and nuns quite openly spoke against him. I witnessed a situation where a Catholic woman, previously a staunch Gallacher supporter but now working for the Labour candidate, insisted on Gallacher having tea in her house as he used to do when he visited Valleyfield, then bursting into tears at the predicament she found herself in.

The anti-communist drive was even carried into the miners' union branches. At an earlier period during the war when we were riding with the stream many of the union branches had taken out shares in the *Daily Worker*. Now, some right-wingers in the union were working to get these holdings cancelled and the money withdrawn. In most cases this was defeated for it was so obvious at the time that the *Worker* was the only daily newspaper speaking out for the miners. Besides, our strongest base was in the miners' union branches. Nevertheless this business took up quite a bit of my time travelling all over the County alerting our miners' groups to this manoeuvre.

Looking back, this must have been a perplexing time for ordinary miners. There were many things in the international arena about Communism that they did not like. It was not just the Tories and the press and radio that were hammering away every day against Communism. The Labour leaders, especially Ernest Bevin, the Foreign Secretary and former trade union leader, were even worse. On the other hand it was the Communists in their own pit and village who were slogging away on the bread and butter issues.

The minimum wage for miners was £5 a week for surface workers and £5 and 15 shillings underground. That certainly did not provide for affluence. In fact dissatisfaction was so rife that the industry was losing miners at the rate of thousands a month. The Labour Government that the miners had voted for with so much enthusiasm only three years earlier had now instituted a freeze on wages. It was the Scottish Area, with Abe Moffat and other Communists in the leadership, who were leading the campaign within the NUM for an end to the wage freeze and an increase for the miners. It was Gallacher in Parliament who was ceaselessly fighting the same battle. And there was absolutely no doubt where the Communist Party in Fife stood. The fight against the wage freeze was at the centre of our campaigning, and we were doing this with such gusto that no one could have been unaware of where we stood. How would the good people of West Fife find their way through this confusing situation when the election came? They were being told such terrible things about the communists yet the ones they knew were quite good fellows.

I am sure that when I first arrived in Fife I took up rather hard-line positions. I wrote to Bridget "The deterioration in communist standards has done a lot of harm... but with a process of Bolshevisation we can make tremendous advances." A little later I was writing "Remember this is a mining constituency and the wages issue is rapidly coming to a head... one of our main tasks is to rouse the militancy and anger of the miners as a basis for a still further swing towards Gallacher." There is no doubt that we really did go to town on wages.

Another daring case was the collection of signatures at some pits to a *Declaration That We Will Never Produce Coal For A War Against Russia.* For myself that declaration came right from the heart, and I know that the same applied to many mining comrades for in the following weeks we had them coming into the office and proudly reporting that they had succeeded in getting their union branch to adopt a similar resolution.

Sometimes this gut feeling got the better of me. Dr. Reid, the production director of the Coal Board in Scotland, had made proposals for the reduction in the number of miners employed in Fife. I drew up plans for a series of protest demonstrations outside his house. This was going a bit far, for although demonstrations were commonplace we never invaded the privacy of anyone's home. When the Scottish miners' leadership learned about this they came down on me like a ton of bricks. They were right. They were far more experienced than I and, besides, they had to do the delicate negotiating to get the best possible solution for their members. With me, rhetoric had taken command.

Then came the real public opinion poll, the County Council elections. They covered a much larger area than Gallacher's constituency, and Fife was largely a farming county though it had a large number of miners concentrated around the pits that were scattered throughout the area. The Council had a typical Scrooge-like Tory majority. A bit earlier I had arranged a deputation in support of a proposal that the children in care should have their weekly pocket money allowance increased from twopence to threepence. They refused to hear the deputation and turned down the proposal. We had four Councillors up for re-election. Two were returned and two lost their seat. Our vote was 5,199 against Labour's 13,126. Almost unbelievably Rab Smith failed to hold his seat in Lumphinnans. This was Moffat territory. Abe had been its representative before Rab. And no one could have been more energetic on behalf of the villagers than Rab. That result shook us.

In Kelty, which had always been a Labour stronghold, John Fernie polled 334 votes to Labour's 1,808. Again, John spent practically all his time doing case work on behalf of Gallacher. He was the person in the constituency most closely identified with Gallacher. Over the years he must have acted on behalf of a lot more people than voted for him. Here is what I wrote about that election at the time:

"I can say this about Fernie's ward: we got every single vote possible. It was the best organised campaign I've ever known. Every house was canvassed. We got 600 definite promises. Every one of these was listed. On polling day they were knocked up two, three and four times until they voted."

No, the votes had nothing to do with the calibre of our candidates or of their standing locally. They were votes against the image of international communism that the Cold War had engraved on the minds of ordinary people.

The General Election was upon us. At least I can say that my work in Fife had done something to activate the members for this moment. We were not short of election workers. We also had comrades from all over the country coming in to help us. Bridget came up from London for the two weeks before polling day. Together we were responsible for Valleyfield and the surrounding villages. Here are the results:

Hamilton, Labour Party; 23,576
Fraser, National Liberal Party; 9,301
Gallacher, Communist Party; 10,131

For me it was shattering. In those days there were no sophisticated voting forecasts and all my time in Fife I had been full out with no time to make arithmetical calculations. It would have made no difference. Nothing could have made the result different in the political climate of that time. At that depressing moment the one thing that sustained me was Gallacher's bearing. Here is what he said when the votes were announced:

"I was a working-class agitator before I went to the House of Commons. I was a working class agitator in the House

of Commons and I still remain a working-class agitator now."

A few sketches of some of the personalities I met in Fife.

ABE MOFFAT: It is not possible to think of Fife of those days without Moffat. He was Fife and he was the miners. His actual position was President of the Scottish Area of the National Union of Mineworkers. He had been a Communist County Councillor for Lumphinnans and was Gallacher's election agent when the seat was won in 1935. He had an imposing appearance: well-built, straight-backed, short cropped bullet head. Puritanical in demeanour, and with a powerful clipped delivery, he was the kind of person you wouldn't take liberties with. Before I went to Fife I used to meet him at the regular gathering of Scottish Party leaders and miners officials. I was there as Lanarkshire Party organiser as we also had a large mining membership. The purpose was to exchange information and views so that we would not have conflicting policies in the coalfield. Being young and with no direct experience in mining I think he looked on me as something of an amateur. I didn't come across him much when I moved into the constituency but on one occasion when I phoned him about something, he was quite offensive to me. That subtracts nothing from his enormous contribution to both the miners and the Communist Party.

LAURENCE DALY: In my early days in Fife, Laurence gave me cause for confidence. After meeting him I wrote an enthusiastic letter about him to Bridget. He was Secretary of the Scottish Miners Youth Council and had just returned from a world conference of some kind. I told Bridget: *"He is secretary of Glencraigs Party branch, 27 years old, and there are about 20 other young miners all around the same age in the branch."* Years later I was interested to notice that Laurence had made the same kind of impact on EP

Thompson, the labour movement historian. In his book *Writing by Candlelight*, he says:

"I know Mr. Daly... Daly is a Fifer... West Fife has had, perhaps, as sophisticated and articulate a political tradition as any in these islands. Daly gained his education in this highly conscious political culture. Whatever may be said about Communist Party policy and organisation... there was then no comparable organisation in which a young miner could enlarge his horizons both nationally and internationally."

Equally interesting about that observation of Thompson's, is the recognition that it was the Communist Party in Fife that gave the grounding for Daly's intellectual development. Laurence left the Party after the Hungarian uprising in 1956. Many years later in the 70s when he was General Secretary of the NUM, I often had a lunchtime drink with him. I regarded him as the most articulate trade union leader of that period and expected he would take over the leadership of the TUC. Then strangely, when he appeared at peak ability, he started to decline quite rapidly. Returning from a Labour conference, he was badly injured in a car crash. That ended his role in the Movement. Laurence remained critical of what he said was my overbearing manner when I was in Fife and alleged that I bullied Jock Penman, a badly wounded International Brigadier, into taking on tasks that were beyond his strength. I don't know whether he was right but I do know Laurence himself was a very humane person.

JOHN FERNIE: I wrote Bridget: *"I cannot finish without saying how I have grown to admire John. There is no one in the Party that I respect more. I cannot say in words what I think of him."* A bit after that John was offered a council house. He could have done with it. He lived along with his wife and two children in an old poorly maintained and inconvenient two-roomed brick house. We had a council of war about this and advised John not to take it, as there were other families in the street who were even worse off than him. We thought that being so near the election this was a ploy by the Labour people on the council to try and discredit him. Both John and Jenny accepted this. When John's old mother heard about this she was furious and rushed down to his house, all guns blazing: *"Be sensible! Think of the children at least!"* Then Jenny came in even angrier: *"My husband has a conscience. He will do what he thinks is right no matter what it means to us."* And the old lady had to retreat. Jenny was such an unselfish person that it never occurred to her that it was she who was making the biggest sacrifice. I remember her as one of the jolliest people I have ever met.

BOB BONNAR: Bob was a young locomotive fireman when I was told about him. When Bridget and I visited him he was nursing his baby son who was terribly marked by chickenpox and crying painfully. In spite of the distractions we recruited Bob that night. We must have made heavy demands on him right from the start, for soon I was writing to Bridget that he was unhappy about leaving his young wife on her own so much. Years later he was elected to the NUR Executive Committee and I re-established contact with him. He was highly regarded in the union for his independent views. On his first day on the Executive he went to the same lodgings as Dan Kelly who was our supremo in the union. Dan said *"I'll take this bed and you take that one."* *"No,"* replied Bob *"We'll vote on it"*. At one stage Bob had to go into hospital for a few weeks. It was the first time in his life that he had time on his hands, so he wrote a novel *Stewartie*. It was about the yearning that newly industrialised workers felt for their rural past. In 1966 the Humboldt University in Berlin published in English a hefty volume of *Life and Literature of the Working Class*, in which Bob has a very moving appraisal of the life and works of James Barke, the Scottish novelist who, incidentally, grew up in West Fife. Sadly, Bob died at a comparatively early age. As I write this I am thinking that if only Bob had been lucky enough to have the leisure time of retirement he would have made a worthy contribution himself to Scottish literature.

COUNCILLOR GEORGE SHARPE: Here is what I wrote to Bridget following my first visit to Thornton, a small railway town. *"There are 15 railwaymen in the branch. A Councillor, George Sharpe, about 30 years of age is the secretary. He is so indescribably good looking that I suppose the women couldn't resist voting for him, and he has a personality and friendliness to match, and intelligence too."* George left the Party at some time and I didn't have further contact with him. But I did see from time to time in the newspapers that he had become quite a distinguished Labour civic dignitary.

COUNCILLOR BOB SELKIRK: Bob was the old veteran Communist of Fife who always held the Party together when things went wrong. He knew everyone and everything about Fife and was one of the two Communist councillors in the small Burgh of Cowdenbeath. After each Council meeting they published and distributed 3,000 copies of a paper about their activities on the Council. Bob was now part of the folklore of Fife. In his younger days he had led a rent strike of Coal Company houses and when they decided to evict them from their tied house, they had to smash down Bob's wall with a tractor.

Chapter 7 - In London –A Militant on the Railway

I moved to London after the general election of 1950 and joined Bridget at her flat at Belsize Park. That was our home for the next 40 years. My first action was to visit the labour exchange in Camden Town. I asked for a job at London docks. That poorly paid civil servant on the other side of the counter was more diligent than his salary required. He noticed that the code number on my insurance card told that I had been a political worker. There was no question of being sent to dockland after that. It has often occurred to me how simple yet sophisticated Britain's surveillance system really is. Whether it is by insurance card or car registration number, the authorities can usually get hold of you.

At that time St. Pancras had a full-time party organiser. He suggested Camden goods depot. The more enterprising rail workers there were leaving in droves for more congenial employment. Thus Camden depot became my official place of work for most of the remainder of my working life. When I went there first, the rail complex consisting of goods depot, locomotive shed and marshalling yard employed around 2,000 workers. Today it no longer exists as a railway establishment. That location now accommodates one of the largest flea markets in London. Every weekend tens of thousands of visitors pass through the gates of the perimeter wall that runs from Chalk Farm to Camden Town. Every time I pass by I think to myself: if only they knew what used to go on here!

In 1872 a bloke called Tarbox got the sack for being in the newly formed Amalgamated Society of Railway Servants. Strikes and rioting throughout the area followed and the railway company was forced to recognise the union. Thereafter, it became firmly established and spread throughout the country.

Being a goods porter was hard physical work. You were a kind of human draught horse pulling a barrow with about a quarter of a ton on it to the loading point, perhaps 100 yards away. This was done at top speed, for a tonnage bonus system of payment operated. You were at this for an eight hour shift with a number of rest spells; otherwise you could not keep up the pace. One of the occupational hazards was a form of foot-rot. You dug your toes into the cement floor to get a good pull. The feet would sweat till the skin became soft and wrinkled, so that if you didn't trim the toe nails properly you ended up with blood-soaked and crippled feet.

I had to get up at five in the morning for a quick breakfast then a sharp 20-minute walk to start work at six. There was a one-hour unpaid meals break in the middle of the day, with a finishing time at three in the afternoon. We had a good parents-collective in our street that shared the taking and fetching of school children. Even so, I would have to do my share once or twice a week.

Even though I would be a bit exhausted and rather grimy at the end of the shift I found this quite a pleasant task. I was going into such a different world, such well-dressed and pretty mums. One of them, the mother of my daughter's best friend, is now a famous authoress.

When I got back with the children there were breakfast dishes to wash, beds to make, the flat to be tidied, and a meal prepared for Bridget coming back at around six in the evening. That was my usual daily programme for 25 years till I was elected to the union executive in 1974.

My wages were far too low to maintain the family and Bridget was the main bread-winner all that time. It certainly was strenuous life for both of us. But that is only half the story. We were both deeply involved in trade union and political activities, which meant that one or both of us were out nearly every evening.

One of my first political acts at Camden depot was to cover the wall with chalked slogans advertising a Dean of Canterbury meeting. It was a silly thing for a new employee to do. I would probably have got away with it in Hamilton, where I was part of the community, but in Camden for a newcomer to behave in such a way, to do something that had not been done before, was looked on by ordinary workers as well as by the supervisors as arrogant. For that misdemeanour, I had to appear before the goods agent and got a very serious dressing down.

I remember that encounter very well. Quite a protocol had to be observed. I was summonsed into the chief clerk's office and from there announced into the inner sanctum, where I was presented to a grim-faced agent with a solemn note-taker by his side. And, because I was not quick enough in showing respect for authority by taking off my cap, the chief clerk swiped it from my head. There was a moment of tension. Fortunately I succeeded in restraining myself. It was a near thing. For many years there was an undeclared war between that goods agent and me.

It expressed itself on one occasion in a rather clumsy way. I had been suffering from boils and my doctor prescribed the wonder antibiotic of that time – since banned – which had the effect of bringing me out in such explosions of eruptions that I had to be rushed into hospital. On the fourth day following, a letter arrived: "Owing to your absence from work for three days without a certificate you are hereby regarded as self-dismissed." My union representative squashed this, like some subsequent charges.

There was another narrow shave. After I had become a bit more established in the depot, I built up a sale of between 30 to 50 *Daily Workers* each day – with a special issue I've gone as high as 100 copies. This had been going on for a few years, then suddenly, just as I was handing a paper to one of my regular readers I was arrested by a couple of British Transport Police who were permanently stationed at the depot. The charge they read out to me referred to a railway by-law, which said that no one was allowed "to sell or exhibit for sale any article on the company's premises without written permission". Obviously that was a frame-up that had been thought up for some time. Again, my union rep, Harry Dowden, got this squashed. One thing that worried me about Harry's handling of the case was that he decided to challenge the by-law with his own alternative legal arguments. His plea was that things should be set in motion to provide for a special dispensation for me. Fortunately, even the top bods were not anxious to become victims of Harry's incisive intelligence and wit.

Harry was a very strange character. He was a real East Ender. He must have been as sharp as a razor as a kid. When he was called up he found himself in the army educational corps. He made full use of this. He was also a prolific reader and would often spice his speeches at mass meetings in the depot with quotes from Shakespeare or Shaw or some other literary figure. It was not done in an affected way and was accepted as quite normal by the workers. In another way he was something of a hermit. He never went to the canteen with the rest of us but had his tea and sandwich by himself in his own little hut. One of his weaknesses was that he could not bear to see anyone in the depot with a higher cultural IQ than himself. We had one such member, Joe Rabstein, who was an accomplished pianist and artist. Harry acquired a violin and practiced all day long. I don't know how good he became because I'm tone deaf. In spite of his peculiarities Harry was practically worshipped by the older men.

One of the things I noticed straight away when I started at Camden was how powerful the local union committee appeared to be. The branch secretary walked about the depot in clean clothes and didn't seem to do very much work. A kind of uneasy balance of power existed between local reps and the management. I think this was because the locally negotiated tonnage pay constituted a big part of the worker's earnings, and management knew that a disgruntled rep could fairly easily get a mass meeting to decide on a work to rule or go-slow. This compelled the agent to establish a rapport with the reps. Often this approach was mutual. At one London depot the reps sponsored a collection for the retiring agent that brought in enough to present him with a grand piano.

When I became tonnage negotiator I always pushed to get as many gangs as possible on to 'grace bonus' – that was a flat payment equal to the average tonnage payment of that particular section. That was because the weight content of the traffic could vary greatly, making it difficult to work out rates that maintained a fair balance between gangs. It also had the effect of easing physical exertion. However, traffic was more and more being switched to road so that ultimately there was none for us.

During the 50s many black workers, mainly from the West Indies, started work on the railway. Some departments were mainly staffed by them. One of these was the shunting yard, which served Camden goods depot. We recruited quite a few of these black shunters into the Communist Party. This was the work of Tony Gilbert, a white comrade who had previously worked in the Yorkshire coalfield. He was the union rep in the shunting yard. I don't think he was more than five feet small but I've never met anyone with more physical or political courage.

Tony was a master of lightning stoppages. By that tactic he had been successful in getting speedy concessions on a whole range of simple demands, such as soap allowance and hand towels, which had become bogged down in the negotiation machinery at a higher level. I'm sure the people at the top had come to the conclusion that Tony's methods could not be allowed to continue indefinitely. At this time the National Front was being born. Its creators were the Webster brothers who had pubs in Camden Town. They started by operating a ban on serving black people in their pubs. Tony and a mixed contingent of black and white shunters would go into one of their pubs and when the blacks were refused drinks all merry hell was set loose.

But the blow against Tony was delivered by railway management. One night shift he and his gang were playing cards in their hut and didn't jump to attention quickly enough to the foreman's orders when a train arrived to be shunted. The disciplinary procedures were applied and Tony was sacked – not the others. His own men came out on strike. I got a mass meeting of the goods workers but even after a savage slogging match, which lasted the whole morning, I failed to get their support. This was due to sectional animosity. Every time Tony's shunters stopped work it affected the earnings of the depot staff. The NUR executives were also unsuccessful in getting Tony reinstated.

For the activist, things don't appear in a simple black and white – a strange metaphor in this instance. Around this time we had recruited a young white loco man. He was intelligent but with the benefit of hindsight there was something unstable about him. Suddenly he began to stir up feeling against the black shunters: you can't see them in the dark, they are a risk to safety, he claimed. As a work problem this was not serious and was put to rest. But coming from one of our own members it was a bit unnerving. We had him expelled from the party.

Let me make another plea to purists and academics. Activists are sometimes confronted with situations that are not settled by rational arguments.

Take this one for instance. One of our Party shunters, a Scotsman, asked me if I would talk with some of his relatives who had just returned from Kenya. They came to our flat; a middle-aged man who had worked on the railway there along with his wife and sister. It was at the time of the Mau Mau events. They asked what I thought about this. I gave them the usual answers about imperialism, national liberation struggles, and the inevitability of unpleasant happenings. Their facial expressions began to show signs of the mental torture they were trying so hard to control. It emerged that one of their children had been a victim of a Mau Mau killing.

Our party rail branch was usually quick to respond to political events. We had a branch meeting – I think eight comrades were present – the night that news was released that Garry Powers American U2 spy plane had been shot down over the Soviet Union. This was a tense moment in the Cold War. We decided to go straight to the American Embassy to protest. The idea was to kick up a bit of a fuss and get some publicity in the hope that it would have a snow-balling effect. On the way we phoned the *Morning Star* of our intentions and asked for a photographer or reporter to go along. When we arrived at the embassy we were discreet: "We must see the Ambassador on a matter of life or death" we said and tried to give it a tone of anxiety and urgency. We gave no hint that it was about the spy plane. It worked. The officials and uniformed guards were uncertain what to do. We were allowed inside. After a time they saw through the ruse. We made a lot of noise. We were playing for time till the photographer turned up. There was a skirmish. One guard went into a room clearly marked 'armoury' and returned with a hand gun. He levelled the gun to my head: "Get out or I shoot. This is American territory," he screamed. There was a moment of tension when everything went quiet. Unbelievable anti-climax: the gun fell from his grasp and went clattering down the marble stairway. After that we were each picked up bodily and thrown out of the building. One of the comrades was Lillian Burgess, a gentle woman rail clerk in Camden. She was wonderful.

Some time later a woman police constable was killed by a shot from a gun fired from the window of the Libyan Embassy. All hell was let loose, quite rightly, in my opinion. But some of it was hysterical, and expressed amazement that any embassy in London should allow guns on its premises. I wrote to the papers about the incident at the American embassy. There was no response.

When I arrived in London in 1950 to join Bridget, Mark was seven years old and Laura five. Josephine, my daughter, was born in February 1951. I think I can say that all three had a happy and exciting childhood. Mark was an exuberant child with no problems. There was a gang of boys in the street, all at the same school, and many of them children of party members. I could watch them from our window, running races or playing football, not a care in the world. To come upstairs to tea was an interruption for Mark to be got over as quickly as possible so that he could get back to rejoin the gang. There is something of that time that remains in him today: he is still a football fanatic, an ardent Arsenal supporter.

Laura was different. From the earliest age she was a wilful character. Not far from our home there was a railway bridge high above the main line into Euston, which we had to pass on our regular Sunday walks to Primrose Hill. She would dash off in front and terrify me by tight-roping along the parapet. The boys and girls in the street had commandeered an empty bomb-site next to our house where they would join together for camp fires, sing songs, and other games. Laura was always prominent in these activities.

Josephine as usual was the lucky one. She learned so much from her brother and sister. One of my fondest memories of their 'one-ness' was the 'Question Time', which often followed our evening meal: one time it would be rivers of the world, the next it would be capital cities. I can still see the sparks jumping out of their eyes as they strained to be first with the answer. The age difference didn't matter. It was an exciting way of learning.

The three of them went to the same primary school, and on the whole enjoyed it. But there was one teacher who struck terror into each one as they progressed into her class. They called her Mrs Syngman-Rhee (the wife of the blood-soaked dictator of South Korea). With such a nickname there is no need for a further description.

Mark moved to the local grammar school, but to our surprise, became increasingly unhappy there. This was unexpected for he was an easy-to-get-on-with sociable young person who took part in the sports activities and had not unreasonable marks in other subjects. We saw the headmaster a number of times. He was a snob; avid to achieve a high score of pupils who made it to university. At one school assembly an announcement was made that pupils who had sold CND badges in the school should report to the headmaster's study. Practically the whole school turned up at his doorstep. That was a red face for him. He should have got a lot more.

When Mark left that school he went to Trent Park Teachers' Training College. What a changed person. He became interested in drama, and has made it his life. With some colleagues he created the 'People Show', the longest running fringe theatre group in the country; it has passed its 21st birthday... and that is something in this arena. But with the current Tory cuts in the Arts who can possibly survive!

Laura went to Parliament Hill Girls' School. She could never do anything by half-measures: her commitment was always total. When she came home from school it would be straight down to homework. One evening when the rest of the family had gathered for dinner Laura was lost. Where could she be? The hours passed and we were becoming more and more worried. There she was at her desk in her own room still in her school uniform poring over her exercise books! Laura had one serious reprimand at school – probably there were others that we never knew about. She had been involved in a protest sit-down in Trafalgar Square and her photograph appeared on the front page of some national newspapers... she had a cigarette in her mouth; that was scandalous, the cause didn't matter.

Laura now lives in the remote mountains of Wicklow in Ireland. She has seven talented children. We see them far too rarely. I've tried to put my feelings about them into verse.

Josephine, again the lucky one, went to Camden Girl's School an excellent educational establishment with sympathetic teachers at that time. She graduated to North London Polytechnic for teachers' training. I remember going to see her there when there was a student occupation in protest at the appointment of a Principal who had some dubious connection with the South African Apartheid Government. This was the time of the Che Guevara cult; they saw every student action as the focal point of imminent world revolution. By that time I was a bit cynical of such prospects. Still, dreams are better than nightmares. Josephine, with husband and three children lives less than a mile away from us. Is it the end of her good fortune?

As a rail worker I got travel concessions for the whole family. This was an enormous plus when the children were young. We are entitled to a certain number of free journeys in Britain and unlimited travel at quarter fare. That concessionary rate applied in France and some other continental countries. When people learn about this they think we are getting something under the counter, a kind of mini-slush payment. All this has been gone into by learned judges during pay enquires. They have calculated the money value of the travel concessions and offset it against our pay claim. The unions have been effective in extending the concessions on the basis of a little bite at a time. I say thanks, for it enabled us, although we were in the lower income bracket, to have some wonderful holidays.

For many years when the children were small we used to go to the Mediterranean, where a friend had a cottage and let us have it free. Bridget and I sat through the 24-hour train journey. It was a bit exhausting. The children were in the corridor in sleeping bags and woke up fresh and bright, though a bit grimy. The pound in the 50s had a high value in France. But you don't need much money when the sun shines every day and there is a warm sea and mountains to climb. In spite of these attractions Josephine developed a strange craze for what she called the 'dead bus', so we had to spend some time outside the cemetery watching the funeral processions going in. One evening just as the light was beginning to fade there were hundreds of people on the beach, all looking out to sea with cameras and binoculars. It was unmistakable. Three sea serpents, each about 30 to 40 feet long were quite visible. There were so many witnesses to this unusual sight, yet there are people who pooh-pooh the existence of our own Loch Ness Monster. We were sad to be told that it was only a school of porpoises.

Years later we switched to camping at the lakes in central France. I've described earlier the load goods porters at Camden were expected to pull. That was baby stuff compared with my burden on these camping expeditions: pots and pans, folding chairs, even an iron camp bed for Bridget's bad back, in addition to tents and all the usual camping gear. I lost so much body-moisture on the trek to the camping site that in spite of drinking gallons of lemonade – it was two or three days before I needed to urinate!

One time we pitched our tent a couple of hundred yards away from the main camp site. There was only one tent next to us, occupied by a quiet but pleasant middle-aged man on his own. He spent most of the time fishing on the lake, apparently thinking his own thoughts. One day the gendarmes came and took him away. Rumour had it that he was a murderer.

Another year Bridget, Josephine and I went to the mountains in Northern Italy. Mark and Laura had outgrown us and were elsewhere with their own friends. Bridget kept pushing us each day to go further and higher up the mountain. Josephine and I were on the point of open revolt when near the summit Bridget fell and sprained her ankle. For us two recalcitrants, it spelt liberation. There would be no more endurance tests for the remainder of the holiday. We skipped down that mountainside singing merrily.

When all children had flown from the nest Bridget and I had camping holidays on our own in Corsica. We would swim in the sea before breakfast, then take the little steam railway up the mountain above Adjaccio and be on the snow-cap of the forest of Vissavona by mid-day. At the campsite there was some disturbance late one night. An intruder on a thieving expedition had been chased but got away. After that the owner of the site and his family took turns throughout the night patrolling with loaded rifles. Some days later the Corsicans were happy. The villain had been caught, not a native, but a young German student who had run out of money. Corsican pride was saved and the traditional enemy dealt with.

In the 50s, we didn't get any travel concessions on the German railways so Bridget and I hitch-hiked to Berlin to see some relatives. On the outward journey we managed a lift most of the way in an empty coal truck. We were black with coal dust and very thirsty. I think the total cost of that journey was the price we paid for a giant melon to slake our thirst. At one place in East Germany we had to present passports for checking – you put your documents through a small window then waited on benches till they were stamped. A militia group made up of both sexes patrolled the building, with machine rifles slung over their arm.

We had sat there for an hour at least, others had been waiting longer. Among them was a well-dressed man, a South American by his appearance. He was getting more and more impatient, paced up and down for a bit, then made the decision. Next minute he was urinating under the passport window. Dead silence. We waited for the rifle shots. No, all that happened was a lot of angry gesticulating by the militia with brooms – about who should wipe up the mess. On the way home it was a Belgian doctor who picked us up. He made a very long detour, his decision not ours, so that we should see the acres and acres of graves in the Ardennes where thousands of young men of the Second World War lay buried. His own emotional wound was still bleeding.

That, as parents, we were able to go off on our own so often was helped by the children belonging to a couple of organisations that provided group activities and camping holidays. One was Forest School Camps. It was the successor of earlier Fabian ideas of open air and healthy living. The camps are manned by volunteers who enjoyed them as children and have come back as adult helpers. Generation upon generation go to them, including our own grand-children. My memory is of the children coming home with wet and mouldy clothing that stank to heaven. It didn't hurt them. They loved it.

The Socialist Sunday School was the other organisation. In addition to cultivating an outlook of peace and racial harmony, there were weekend hikes in the Chilterns, which were easy to reach from the Finchley Road station. Another popular activity was the drama group. We were very lucky in Hampstead to have Marjory Mason, herself a well-known actress, to do the coaching. Our bunch always got first prize at their annual festival. It was here that Mark's interest in theatre began.

Now that we are oldies, we have holidayed in Scotland for the past ten years, walking at a more leisurely pace and fishing for wild brown trout. In spring this year (1991) we visited Sir David Steel's Ettrick Water on the borders. What an attractive river! But I fished it morning, noon and night for a week and didn't even see a minnow. In the summer we went for our first time to Wester Ross and then on to the Torridon Mountains in Sutherland. In the two weeks I caught at least a couple of hundred trout. We had them fried, baked, grilled, and even made into a pate to put on toast. Back home we are now on sausages.

For a number of years we also holidayed in beautiful Kerry in the south of Ireland. On one of these we had been boat fishing on Clooney Lake, when in disembarking; Bridget fell back and struck her ribs on the oarlock. At the time it was very painful but we thought she had only suffered a bad bruise. A couple of days later she became quite ill. I had to drive her the 12 miles into Kenmare to the nearest doctor. After examining her he phoned for her to be admitted straight away to Bantry Hospital. Apparently she had broken a rib, which had penetrated a lung and an infection had developed. Her condition was serious. A thousand times I have re-enacted that 50-mile journey over the mountains to Bantry, every few seconds stealing a glance at Bridget. She was failing fast. I feared she would pass out before I got there. We were just in time. At the hospital they pumped her full of penicillin.

Each day for the next week I did that journey to Bantry then back in the evening when it was getting dark. I got to know every stone in the way and to hate every sheep that refused to rise from the middle of the road. Have you ever seen sheep's' eyes in the glare of car headlights? They seem to be made of glass. They throw back a reflection. But it is as though there is nothing behind the eyes. It is quite uncanny.

For much of the time in hospital Bridget was only semi-conscious. The one thing that has remained in her mind is a nurse asking her "What do you want, Mass or porridge?" A strange choice for a communist of Jewish origin in such a state! As for me, a communist of Scottish upbringing, I am quite clear: that Catholic hospital saved Bridget's life. I don't know words to adequately acknowledge that debt.

Chapter 8 - Communist Parliamentary Candidate

My first Party assignment as a 'Londoner' was to carry the portable speakers' platform from our premises in Camden High Street to Warren Street Tube Station which was being tried out as a site for Saturday afternoon open air meetings. The speaker was to be Jock Kennedy, an official in the plumbers union. I was to learn that he got into every speech that he used to spend a lot of time in the Queen's bathroom. Apparently, when he was a journeyman he had been in charge of some job in Buckingham Palace. He always got a laugh from his audience when he said. "And I can tell you, she sits on that seat I put in for her more than she sits on old George's throne." But I am digressing. Back, to Warren Street Tube Station.

I got there well before the meeting was due to start. While I was waiting a strange thing happened. A man came out of the station with two women on his arms. He introduced them to a couple of men who had been hanging about the entrance. They all disappeared. Ten minutes later the same thing happened all over again. I was just beginning to cotton on when he emerged again, but this time the woman refused to go with the client and there was a scuffle with blows and screams. I was trying to make up my mind whether to intervene when just at that moment a policeman approached and came over to me: "I hope you are not going to cause any trouble this afternoon," he said. "Just look over there," I replied. The copper was furious and grabbed me by the lapels: "I'll have you if you're not careful." I realised that it was us he objected to not the pimps.

From 1950 to the mid 70s – a quarter of a century – I was a super-activist. There were some others like me, but not that many. I had to do my eight hours hard manual labour at Camden goods depot every weekday as my contribution to the household expenses. For most of that time I was also the local union rep on the depot. That involved dealing with issues that often caused me anxiety and tension. In addition, I was on the London District Council of the union and its executive committee; that took up at least two evenings a month. On top of this I was on the London District Committee of the Party. I was secretary of the Rails Party branch and active in ward branch activities. What a list! None of these were honorary positions. They all required time and involvement. It meant that I had very few evenings or weekends at home.

In the four general elections: 1955, 59, 64, and 66, I was the Communist Parliamentary Candidate in the North St. Pancras Constituency. I was also a candidate in four Borough Council elections and once for the Greater London Council (GLC); that was nine contests in 12 years. I have one of my election addresses before me now. The blurb on the front says: "Jock Nicolson is a familiar figure to the people of St. Pancras, both during and between elections." That was no exaggeration.

In these Parliamentary Elections, I polled between 1,140 (the lowest) and 1,303 (the highest) votes. In 1959 Bill Webster, who became one of the founders of the National Front, stood as a so-called National Labour Candidate and polled 1,685 votes against my 1,230 and Labour's 22,256. The write-up in *The Times* summarised Webster's programme as: "Against coloured immigration, for a union of the white dominions and Western Europe as a third force."

This was a rumbustious election campaign right from the beginning, and I must confess I was the first one to wrong foot things. At a Saturday afternoon meeting at Queens Crescent I described Webster as a "punch-drunk, second-rate boxer" - (he had been a boxer in his younger days). This was perhaps one of the most reckless statements I have ever made, for many of the market-stall holders there were his toughest supporters. I can't remember how I extricated myself from that gaffe but it taught me not to make such wild statements. During that election, meetings were well attended and often rowdy and even at the counting of the votes Webster was involved in a scuffle. By then he was being cold-shouldered by all the other candidates and organisations in the Borough. Open racism was not respectable.

Electioneering was heavy going. It meant canvassing round the council flats and working class streets with the *Morning Star* most Sundays, and on week-nights during the summer. We didn't limit this to three weeks before an election, but kept it going as a regular activity. On a Saturday afternoon I would do street meetings at Queens Crescent or Kentish Town station. But with increasing traffic it became more and more difficult to be heard above the noise. This led to the craze for amplifiers. But we soon learned you couldn't present a reasoned case over these things. All you can do is to shout at people and in any case most of them are too busy on a Saturday afternoon to listen. One election I tried to get over this problem. I went round the main streets with a portable loudspeaker, accompanied by Miss X, a professional singer with a very powerful voice. She would sing a couple of verses over the loudspeaker. It certainly attracted attention and people would halt at this unusual happening then I would take over, shout a few selected slogans and try to get in the punch line "AND DON'T FORGET TO VOTE FOR JOCK NICOLSON, THE COMMUNIST CANDIDATE" before they realised what was going on and moved off.

Of all the communist candidates in the country, mine were always among the best results. No wonder, in North St. Pancras we had such a talented team: Doctor Wally Davis, Hugh Falconer, Tony Ryle (cousin of Martin Ryle, the astronomer), Ralph Millner, the first communist QC, Sam Aaronovitch and many others. Still, we remained at the bottom of the poll. Much more serious, our vote continued to decline as the years went on. Why did we keep going for so long? One reason is that once a candidate is adopted it starts something that has momentum. What we were concerned with was not just votes but campaigning amongst the people and elections gave us that opportunity. We knew our votes would not be high. But we were dead serious about getting our message across because we were dead serious about our mission.

Some of the most dramatic protest actions of the post-war period were the rent riots in St. Pancras in 1959 and 1960. The Tories had won a majority on the Council and decided to increase rents. At that time Council rents were around £3 or £4 on average. We organised meetings in all the Council blocks and called on the tenants to refuse to pay the increase. To stir them up I warned" "If the Tories get away with it this time rents will ultimately reach £10 a week." I thought that I was probably overdoing it but look at rent levels now!

Month after month Council meetings were brought to a halt by massive protest demonstrations inside and outside the town hall. Scuffles and arrests were numerous. On one occasion a regiment of police cavalry who had been concealed in Somerstown rail yard were released on the demonstrators when they got the upper hand of the police cordon around the building. Camera crews from all over the world came to capture the drama and excitement of some of these events.

Tenants associations were formed in all the blocks and met every week. After long discussions a strategy was agreed. From a number of volunteers two tenants were selected who would refuse to pay any rent, and their flats would be fortified against the bailiffs. The two chosen were Arthur Rowe in Hampstead Road in the south of the borough, and Don Cook at Kenniston House in the north. It was particularly heroic of Don for he had a young family at the time. Both Arthur and Don were members of the Communist Party. Arthur was a dining-car attendant at Euston and Don worked on London Transport.

I had overall responsibility for the defence at Kenniston House. Kenniston House is a four-storey tenement type building of about 100 flats. It stands on three sides of a rectangular courtyard, with huge iron railing with a gate on the fourth side alongside the road. This gate is the sole entrance. Don's flat was on the top floor on the corner high above the road. It was perfectly sited for our purpose.

The initiative and inventiveness of the tenants was amazing. There was a place nearby where old pianos were dumped; they must weigh near half a ton. These were hoisted on to the balconies so that every stairway could be blocked at a moments notice. Someone else got a supply of lighthouse flares. In all the blocks there were a variety of warning systems so that tenants could be called out at any time, day or night. There was a 24-hour picket at both fortifications. This alert continued over a number of weeks.

I was going past one day and was quite amused to watch a couple of policemen plead with the pickets for permission to enter the flats to serve a summons on some youngster who had been up to some mischief. Eventually they were allowed in under escort.

The siege of the two flats continued for many weeks during which time there were many demonstrations to the Town Hall. Invariably these ended up in rowdy scenes and clashes with the mounted police. News and camera teams from many parts of Britain and abroad reported these clashes in the press and television. Arthur Row's flat at Silverdale, which fronted on the main road near Euston Station became something of an attraction for tourists and amateur photographers. Arthur was a bit of a showman and knew how to respond. When crowds gathered he would lower a bucket by rope from his high-up window to receive the food and good things well-wishers brought him to show their solidarity. On one of these occasions my daughter Josephine, who was eight years old, was thrilled to be the centre of attention when Arthur lowered the bucket with a bar of chocolate in it as a special present for her.

Eventually 'D' Day did arrive. It happened about five o'clock in the morning. About 500 policemen were mobilised against each site. Our response was carried out according to plan. The flares went up and the alarms rang out. Within minutes hundreds of people began to assemble at both sites. My own depot came out on strike that morning. All day long, building sites downed tools as they heard the news and marched to Hampstead Road and Kenniston House to show their solidarity. The atmosphere was electric.

Entry was made by means of a powerful extending ladder manned by unknown individuals and protected by a solid square of policemen. The slates were ripped off and the roof smashed in. Don and his family were resolute, only numbers overpowered them. I was arrested right at the start in the first clashes with the police and taken to Holmes Road Jail. That afternoon I appeared before a magistrate and there to my amazement was a witness against me whom I recognised as one of the regular attendees at the weekly tenants meetings. I had always noticed him. He was better dressed, always took notes but never spoke. I assumed he was from one of the posher blocks of flats and felt a bit uncomfortable in that very proletarian gathering, so I always made a point of giving him a friendly nod or handshake. Now the penny dropped. He was an under-cover policeman and these notes were to incriminate me. The Police wanted an adjournment so that they could prepare a conspiracy charge. For some reason that I could not follow, the magistrate refused to go along with that and I was dealt with under a lesser charge and fined.

Parallel with the rent campaign a sharp struggle was taking place in St. Pancras' Labour Party between the left wing and the right. John Lawrence had become leader of the Labour group on the council. He had a Trotskyite background and had been employed by the Ford shop stewards to produce their combine factory newspaper. I had never really known what the word 'charisma' meant till I met him. With that gift he soon built up a substantial following among the councillors and activists in the Labour Party. He worked closely with us in the rent campaign. His journalistic experience combined with access to St. Pancras council's financial affairs enabled him to show the large proportion of rent that went to pay the moneylenders. Rarely has the robbery of the poor by the rich been so graphically demonstrated as in the leaflets and material that were produced for that campaign. It was an important factor in the exceptional mobilisation of St. Pancras tenants.

John's main opponent in the Labour Party was Councillor Peggy Duff. She wasn't right wing; in today's terminology she would be classified as 'soft left', but she was a paranoiac anti-communist and opposed to John's collaboration with us. Later on, Peggy was CND's organiser of peace spectaculars, but during the rent struggles her aim was to win control of the tenants' movement. But that tough political manipulator had to work with caution for her own daughter, Alderman Cathy Sherridan, was the principal liaison between John's group and the Communist Party. John's right-hand man was councillor Jock Stallard. In the 1975 General Election Jock was one of Harold Wilson's minders. He is now Lord Stallard, a life peer.

John was expelled from the Labour Party, the charge being that he shared a platform with Jock Nicolson, a well-known communist. He then joined our Party along with Cathy Sherridan and some other councillors and trade-union activists including Bernie Holland, who was at that time a shop stewards' leader in the big Covent Garden market. Their membership lasted only a few years. A couple of years ago I was to see John on the opposite side of the street, all dressed up like a Tolstoyan character: long hair, flowing beard, and sandals. I'm sure he will be strikingly different right to the end.

In the period of full employment after the war, tens of thousands of rail workers left the industry for better pay and conditions elsewhere. British Rail had to go abroad to recruit labour from Poland and Italy to fill the gap. Then, in 1951, they offered existing employees a monetary reward for each individual they could bring on to the railway. Just at that time the *Daily Mirror* was running a series of articles about a certain Jock McInawe, a railway platelayer in Southend, who left the railway because he had too much tea to drink and too little work to do. The truth was a bit different. McInawe changed from the railway to a private contractor to get unlimited overtime and Sunday work. For railway employees overtime was restricted in the interests of safety, but that did not apply to contractor's employees.

One night, while interest in this story was high, I took half a dozen of our members to the *Daily Mirror* armed with the railway recruiting leaflet. We managed to get past the security people at the door and up to the floor where there were dozens of journalists banging away at typewriters. We went round inviting each one to fill up the application form on the leaflet, telling them in a very loud voice that they wouldn't need to work so hard and they would get plenty tea. Pandemonium broke out. Deadlines were being missed. Soon a suave young man came up and offered to take us to the editor. He politely opened a door and ushered us in; it was the lift not the editor's office. We plunged down to earth. This time the security men were not deceived, so we got a hard kick on the arse to help us on our way.

In spite of staff shortages, especially in my own goods and cartage sector, we have often taken a negative attitude to sensible changes that rail management has attempted to introduce. We were against palletisation, a very simple improvement, on the grounds that it might mean fewer jobs. How often have I waxed lyrical about the superiority of the antiquated sack barrow! We were against a link with Post Office parcels: they might benefit instead of us by taking over some of our work.

We refused to allow nationalised road transport into some of our depots; road transport, we suspected, might supersede the rail wagon. I suppose there is some excuse for us; we lacked education. After all, the top transport experts got it wrong as well. They allowed Beeching to do so much damage. Now we have nightmare transport on both road and rail. And the present Tory transport ideas about privatising the railways and applying free-for-all market principles to transport is too stupid for even us uneducated louts.

I confess that some of the positions we took up were totally indefensible. For example: the railways had a number of motor driving schools which had originally been established to train horse carters, where there had been a switch from horse-drawn lorries to motor vehicles for the collection of freight from traders in the high street to be taken to rail terminals for transit by rail to their final destination. Now, with the staff shortage, anyone from the labour exchange could get two weeks intensive training on basic pay at these schools if they said they would work on the railway.

What often happened was that once they gained their driver's license they opted to work for a private company. This became such a financial haemorrhage that management proposed that in those cases the one weeks' 'lying time' pay would be forfeited. We refused to allow it, thus putting the nationalised rail industry in the position of subsidising its chief competitor.

A similar situation applied in the hotels sector. One weeks' training with pay and hostel accommodation was given to chambermaid recruits. Every girl in the remotest village in Ireland knew about this. What an opportunity to look around for digs and another job in labour starved London. Again the railways were the Fairy Godmother.

The experimentation for containerised rail transport was carried out at a sub-depot of Camden. The problem was to find the right kind of crane for lifting containers from rail wagons. Mr White, a professional engineer was in charge of the project. Our depot had to supply the men to learn to work the crane. Some of our most competent men went for training but came back depressed and dissatisfied; they had all been classified as 'unsuitable'. After getting a lot of complaints about the surly Mr. White, instead I decided to go myself and investigate first hand. The crane was mounted on giant aircraft wheels and straddled the running line. It bounced rather than ran on these great inflated tyres. The manipulation of the arms and other movements was by a set of levers on a complex panel. I confess I found it all very confusing after being accustomed to nothing more complicated than a sack-barrow and when the time came to be tested I made sure beforehand that I would be called away on union business that day.

I thought that I must have been aiming too high, up in the clouds in that crane, so I decided to be a bit more down to earth, and went to our driving school at Watford to train on articulated lorries. The difficult part is in being able to reverse into a narrow alley-way but with artics' you have to steer the opposite way from where you want to go. This seemed daft to me, and the proof was that the others whom I classified as completely mad thought nothing of it and passed the test. As for me? I decided on the intelligent thing and bought a bicycle. Thereafter, Bridget and I had some wonderful trips in the countryside. All had not been lost.

Chapter 9 - In the Union Leadership

Right from the moment of coming to London I was active in trade union work as well as being involved in local party activity. Union branch meetings in the big goods depots were not well attended; the LDC reps (shop stewards) were always available on the depot to handle grievances as they arose. It was only a small core of activists who attended, and most of them were only interested in their own sector and not in the more general affairs of trade unionism or political questions. Very soon I became our branch delegate to the London District Council of the NUR.

At that time it had a large membership and many branches and there would be anything from a hundred delegates upwards attending the monthly council meeting. Some were there to push the particular causes they were interested in and others to become known and climb the union ladder.

One of the most articulate delegates was Sid Bidwell. I took him to be a Trotskyite and we clashed frequently, usually on political matters. Sid became a Labour College lecturer and later Labour MP for Southall. He always spoke up strongly for the large black and Asian community there. But as I write this, Sid, at 73 years of age, is facing attempts by some in these groups to have him de-selected.

In my early days on the District Council, Arthur Green from Stratford Rail Workshop was President, and the most competent chairman of an assembly I've ever served under. He had to be. With so many delegates all demanding their say he had to show firmness, objectivity and tact all in the right proportions to be able to get through an agenda. Nowadays trade union meetings are not nearly so well attended.

Tom A'herne who was chairman of the Earls Court Branch at that time was the undisputed leader of our Party rail groups in London. Tom had a somewhat similar background to myself. His wife came from a highly respected family of Jewish intellectuals. I worked very closely with Tom until he retired. At a memorial meeting to Tom when he died, I tried to assess his contribution. I said something like this: "In the folklore of our Movement some people achieve greatness through one single heroic act. That is the easier way. Tom A'herne was different. He won such wide recognition because of his consistency and dedication over such a long period."

I keep thinking about this. There are great historical characters like Lenin or Stalin who change human society. Then there are their disciples who keep the change on course. Both are part of a single process. But it is the disciples who make the process a reality, and lasting.

I became secretary of the District Council. It came about like this: the council executive of which I was a member became involved in an unofficial strike movement on London Transport. Sid Hoskins who had been council secretary for many years, took up an ambivalent position, the strike was on, then off, then on again. It was only partially supported by the men on the job but caused the biggest seize-up that London had known. There was strong feeling on the District Council about Sid's indecisiveness and when the annual election came round I defeated him by one vote. Sid was terribly upset and demanded that the delegates be checked against the register. It was found that in the case of Eddie Wynn, delegate from Euston branch, that his branch secretary had failed to send in his name. This was not uncommon but Eddie's vote was disqualified, and Sid remained Secretary. Sometime later he gave up the position and I took over.

I mentioned Eddie Wynn. I had a lot of respect and admiration for him. He was a great big Welshman who had gone to Canada during the depression to look for work. He became friend and bodyguard to Tim Buck, general secretary of the Canadian Communist Party. The political situation there was much more violent than in Britain and in an unemployed demonstration Eddie got bashed about a bit and landed in jail for a year. He came back to Britain and drifted to Euston where he became union rep in the dining-car stores.

Danny Gibbons was another union rep on Euston station at that time. He was an International Brigader, and arising from the knocking about he had suffered was not in good health. Kath, his wife, was the best woman speaker I had in my propaganda team when I stood as Parliamentary candidate in North St. Pancras. She was a very caring person and always appealed to the heart. The last time I saw her she was doing social work for Camden Borough Council. Another International Brigader was Bosco Jones who worked in the Left Luggage Office on King's Cross station.

While I was secretary of the district council, Bill Riordan was president for much of the time. He was a Party member but never pushed politics in the council. He came from a very highly respected railway family. His daughter was Railway Queen one year, and was prominent in the movement to raise money for the railway orphans' homes. His brother-in-law, Alf Press, was a leading member of the loco men's union in London. Bill also held the position of National Treasurer of the NUR. This was an office that had been carried over from the early days of the union. Every cheque in the name of the NUR had to be signed by Bill. He got every Friday off work to do this. It was a prestigious position. My problem with Bill was that he was a heavy smoker. He had a little pipe that was continuously lit; his index finger was actually square at its tip from ramming tobacco into the bowl. Either my eyes would be streaming or I would have a smoke screen in front of me, or on the very rare occasions when Bill put his pipe on the table I was sure to put my hand on the red-hot bowl. Sadly, Bill was run over by an engine at work and killed.

Another very sad story is that of Jim Prendergast. Jim at the age of 16 was a disciple of Jim Larkin in Dublin and was already on the soap box. He went to Spain and fought in the Irish Battalion of the International Brigade. He spent a year at the Comintern school in Moscow. During the war he was the guinea pig in some of Professor Haldane's experiments on submarine pressure. He became a passenger guard at Marylebone station and was elected to the union's Executive Committee. Unfortunately Jim had a health condition so that the smallest quantity of alcohol knocked him over. One evening Molly, Jim's wife, phoned me to say that Jim hadn't come home and she was worried for he had not been well that day. I went off immediately and called at all the places I could think of, but no luck. While I was looking for him, Jim was actually not far from his own home. He had sat on the garden wall before going in and had fallen and struck his head on the hard pavement. He never regained consciousness. I still have the copy of the *Red Flag* that was sung at Jim's funeral. It is only a piece of paper, but to me... it is a memorial to an old comrade and friend.

It may be appropriate here to talk about alcoholism. I maintain that it is an occupational hazard for our trade union executive members. This is particularly the case for those representing the London area. The ones from Scotland and other outlying districts go back to their lodgings and have a proper meal and a quiet evening. Not so for the London representatives, they are expected to visit branches and be involved in other union activity. Often it means rushing off from Unity House at the end of an EC meeting without having had a meal or hanging about in a pub for an hour. On top of this there is always the factor of tension, wondering whether you made the right decision on an important issue. I know that when I was on the executive committee my health was much poorer than when I had to do hard manual labour. Of course, the purist can say "stick to lemonade". Fortunately the world is not made up of such cranks.

District council secretary was a lay position for which I was allowed off work for two days a month to prepare minutes and other material. My equipment was an old typewriter, duplicator, and a heavy iron machine called an 'Addressograph' which must have predated Stephenson's Rocket. Bridget had just bought a posh carpet. Her job involved visiting the docks, and she got it there at a knock-down price as part of a damaged cargo. It was blue and had such a thick pile that it was a sensuous experience to walk through it bare-foot. But it began to change colour, first to mauve, then even darker. Bridget said it was the salt water coming through. I supported that explanation and prayed that it wouldn't dawn on her that it was sparks of printers' ink that flew from my antiquated equipment.

I have written mainly about Communist personalities, but it is necessary to get the balance correct. At no time were Communists the dominant or majority influence at any level in the NUR; far from it. There were many magnificent Labour Party and non-party stalwarts who played an equal or greater part than anyone I've mentioned. In fact, most of the campaigns and activities in which we were involved were initiated by these individuals.

We did meet from time to time as communists in the railway industry. Usually this involved members from all of the rail unions, and sometimes we would have researchers with us, but these meetings were generally for the purpose of working out policy for the industry and we often published policy statements as pamphlets or as articles in the *Morning Star*. Some of these appeared over my name. I must have been much more self-confident then than I am now. This was no different from Labour Party practice, except that they were more professional than us. We also met from a wider trade union constituency to discuss major questions such as incomes policy, etc., but again that is no different from other parties and there is nothing subversive about it. When we spoke publicly or on behalf of our respective unions we expressed the official policy of the union and not the policy of the Communist Party.

I would never allow it to be said that because we were interested in the bigger issues of the movement that we were less concerned with the immediate everyday problems of the membership. Speaking personally, I am sure that no such accusation has ever been entertained against me at any level in the union. On the depot, for example, I negotiated tonnage payments. Increasingly, management brought in more professional work-measurement teams and I had to match this with all the intelligence (and cunning) that I could muster. I would go round the gangs beforehand and tell them to ease the pace but it was difficult to get them to do so for any length of time, they were so accustomed to work at the speed that brought them in the highest earnings.

While I was district council secretary almost all our energy was taken up in carrying out the decisions of the national executive committee of the union. From 1950 onwards there was one pay crisis after another. Then there was the restructuring of the industry: from steam to diesel then to electric propulsion and the massive changes to grading structure and working practices that that involved. There was the Beeching era of cuts, and since then, even more drastic dismemberment and closing down of whole sectors of the industry. In the NUR, the district council is the main forum for explaining these changes and executive policy on them.

During my term of office I must have arranged many dozens of meetings for EC members to report on these issues, and organised the distribution of hundreds of thousands of leaflets from union headquarters. And re-member, all this was done on a voluntary basis without pay other than the two days a month already referred to. I don't think it is an empty boast to say that the North London District Council under my steward-ship was one of the best in the country. It was also the training ground for some of the finest of the next generation of NUR leaders: John Cogger, later National President; Alan Norman, later an officer responsible for London Transport; Tony Donaghy, Executive Committee member and many others.

I was elected to the Executive Committee (EC) of the NUR for the term 1974/75/76; then in accordance with rule I had to stand down for the following three years, and was re-elected for 1980/81/82. My time on the EC coincided with Sidney Weighell's period as General Secretary (GS), 1975 to '82. The NUR has a highly centralised structure. All levers of power are in the hands of the GS; all officers at national and district level and the entire office administration are responsible to the GS and not to the EC. The EC can only deal with matters laid before it by the GS. They cannot take any initiative on their own, and in fact, can't insist on getting information from the office staff unless it is OKed by the GS.

When I was still green on the EC I got a lot of assistance from Frank Cannon, an Assistant General Secretary (AGS). He put me wise to the situation: "It is not what the GS puts before you but what he doesn't that is important," he told me in confidence. Another AGS, Charlie Turnock, was the exact opposite. He was the only officer I could not get on with. On one occasion we were together at the Fashion Flow Company. We were having a chat with the managing director before starting formal business. I had been tutoring on that company's disciplinary procedures at our union school, and I asked the manager if he would let me have any statis-tics they had on this. It would have been useful teaching material. No problem was the reply. At this Charlie jumped in a very aggressive man-ner and told the manager "You will do no such thing. The channel of communications with this union is direct to our head office." The Man-ager had the grace to retire and leave the floor to Charlie and me to f*** it out for the next five minutes.

Charlie had been a commando during the war. He couldn't change. When I went with Frank Cannon to negotiate with National Carriers and we weren't making progress, Frank would say to them: "Next time I won't come. I'll let Charlie off the leash on you". That got smiles, but not better results. Yet Sid Weighell did some not so pretty things to get Charlie to succeed him and keep Jimmy Knapp out of the GS's seat.

When Weighell took office in 1975 it was not just a breath of fresh air, it was something of a whirlwind that swept through Unity House. Dave Bowman had been elected President the previous year. He was a former Communist Party member and had been on the CP's Executive Committee but left the party over some disagreement about trade-union policy. (NUR rules debarred a Communist from holding that particular office). Bowman and Weighell certainly made a very lively pair. Bowman hoisted the slogan: "The union is under new management now." That is how many of us felt at that time after the rather dreary reign of Sid Greene, the previous GS. John Cogger and I went round the London branches popularising that view in an effort to generate enthusiasm.

Weighell should get full credit for the many positive changes he brought about. The old Unity House was rebuilt – the spare space provided letting accommodation – and benefited the NUR financially. He started up a residential school to train our local representatives. He strengthened the NUR's representation in Parliament. He streamlined communications with branches and individual members so that they got much more detailed information about negotiations than they ever had before. He improved expertise in many areas, especially in relation to transport policy. He was masterly as a negotiator. The finest coup de grace I ever witnessed was his handling of the closed-shop negotiations on British Transport Hotels. He won, and left that stubborn management like a litter of paper bags.

In the September 1976 issue of *Labour Monthly*, I had an article entitled 'NUR awakes!' Here is the first paragraph:

"It is just over a year since Sidney Weighell took over the general secretary ship of the National Union of Railwaymen on the retirement of Lord Greene, and at this year's annual conference in July he was amply able to demonstrate that already a whole series of initiatives had been taken to shake the NUR. out of its torpor of recent years and turn it into a 'pacemaker' on the railways and in the trade union movement generally."

It must also be said that Sid's seven years as GS was a very difficult one, especially the last two years when Thatcher was Prime Minister, and just at that time the rail industry ran into a very serious financial crisis. This resulted in the Rail Board and the Government coming forward with a series of drastic measures: closure of rail lines and workshops, large scale redundancies, changes to grading and working practices etc. This was probably the biggest shake-up the railways had known since the Beeching era. Sid responded with energy and imagination. To every move made by the Board or Government he put forward an alternative. And they were carefully thought out and rational alternatives.

In all this he was something of a human dynamo. I think his early football training taught him to move fast and shoot straight. He jumped from one issue to another with such speed that it was often difficult for Executive Committee members to keep pace with what he was up to. I've already mentioned that the NUR was a very highly centralised union with all information and communications firmly in the hands of the GS and not the Executive. On top of this Sid had a very strong authoritarian streak in his make-up and it often looked as though he wanted to be a one-man band. I think this contributed to a certain uneasiness among EC members about Sid's moves.

Sometimes we were quite justified in being suspicious. This came back to me when I read his book in 1983. There, he said, at an early stage in the negotiations with British Rail about making financial savings we were ready to co-operate with them on the "Withdrawal of the collection and delivery of parcels". I was surprised at that statement and certainly have no recollection of agreeing to that. In fact, it would have been very difficult for me or my colleagues who directly represented the 2,500 parcels motor drivers concerned to voluntarily support a strategy which amounted to sacrificing them in order to save some different sector of the workforce.

The political turmoil that wracked the NUR from 1980 to 1982, and ultimately brought Weighell down had very largely himself to blame. He says in his book that along with some other trade-union leaders they decided to drive what he called the 'hard left' out of the Labour Party and the unions. The intensification of the Right versus Left struggle was their decision. And Sid, with his temperament and personality could never do things by half measure. In fact, anyone reading his book or articles he wrote at that time will find it difficult not to come to the conclusion that he had become quite paranoid. What extravagant language he uses! He admits to 'belligerent attacks' on the Left. He put the spotlight on the activities of the Militant Tendency but there was plenty of venom for others on the Left, especially Tony Benn. On the other hand, he had a soft touch for the extreme Right in the Labour Party, David Owen, Shirley Williams and William Rodgers, even when they broke away and formed the Social Democratic Party.

Sid was quite ruthless in the methods he used to get his own way. At the 1980 TUC he voted for a referendum on the Common Market contrary to NUR policy. Some members of the delegation complained to the EC. At first he stalled in bringing the correspondence before our sub-committee and we didn't get it until June 1981. Even then we went out of our way to present a conciliatory report, which simply said: "The NUR vote should have been cast for the resolution to get out of the Common Market and not for the amendment for a referendum." In moving this sub-committee report I stressed that we did not want this to become a personal matter.

Up to his last year I had a reasonable relationship with Sid. In fact the only time I heard him crack a joke was when he was using me as a kind of Aunt Sally to bounce his witticisms off. At our 1978 Annual Conference Arthur Stroud was sitting next to me. We were both running for the EC and Arthur leaned over and whispered: "I wish he would give me as much publicity as you get from him."

But increasingly Sid saw himself as the hammer of the Left, not only in the union, but in the Labour Party and the TUC as well. When Ken Livingstone became leader of the Greater London Council (GLC), there was an almost immediate attack on him by Weighell. I was on London Transport sub-committee of the EC at the time and was quite bewildered by this. But the explanation comes out in his book: "Under Livingstone the GLC seems to be more interested in political warfare with the Tory Government and embarrassing the Labour Party leadership than in running transport in the capital." We have always had a close relationship with the NUM no matter who was in the leadership but when Arthur Scargill became their President that ended. Sid says: "I found it impossible to work with him."

Our relations with ASLEF have always been dodgy, but in the very difficult situation that all the rail unions found themselves in 1982, we should have been doing everything possible to keep together. Instead, Weighell launched a particularly vicious media attack on ASLEF leader Ray Buckton. Sid says: "We had no personal contact and during my eight years as NUR General Secretary I only once went to ASLEF's headquarters…"

When tempers were at their worst between the two General Secretaries I took a collection in our NUR Negotiating Committee and we all went across to Euston Station where I presented a £100 cheque to Albert Williams, ASLEF branch secretary there. It was a token action to try and take the heat out of the situation at local level. My picture, making the presentation, was on the front page of *The Sun* and the *Morning Star*. In his book, Sid says he kicked up merry hell about this. If so, he must have fired high above my head. I have no recollection of getting a dressing down. And that would be unusual, for anyone who came into Sid's line of fire generally had a deep wound to show for it.

Weighell saw 'Reds under the bed' everywhere – even where they didn't exist. Our 1979 Annual Conference was held in St. Andrews, and Militant Tendency supporters in the University there issued their usual silly leaflets to delegates attacking the union leadership and presenting their prescriptions for instant revolution. They organised a fringe meeting but not a single delegate attended. Nevertheless, Sid used this to start up a totally unnecessary campaign about 'Unofficial Circulars and other literature by unauthorised bodies'. Actually, not one of our 26-man EC had any time for the Militant Tendency and their influence at branch or district level was insignificant. In the end only three members in the whole of the union were charged with distributing this unofficial material. Sid made a mountain out of this and a sub-committee of the EC was set up to go into this matter. I was a member and an enormous amount of time was spent on it. In the end we recommended that no action be taken as the members concerned would claim that they were only exercising their civil rights. This was accepted by a majority of the EC, though some who were in the CP voted against that recommendation.

This business came before the following Annual Conference of the union. Sid had sent out an enormous volume of correspondence to branches about Militant Tendency activities directed towards the union. He drew attention to articles in their newspaper attacking some aspects of union policy. They had circularised some branches with their propaganda and tried to win members and set up groups among railwaymen to further their policy. He claimed that 50 branches and district councils had responded to his correspondence expressing disagreement with Militant, and by implication the 'no action' decision of the Executive Committee.

...It was my responsibility at that Conference to defend the Executive's decision. But right at the start of the debate Sid had this to say:

"I have been buying the *Morning Star* from our colleague here (me) and I have a subscription to Brother Nicolson to a fighting fund for the *Morning Star*. I have every respect for them. They are a separate political party who have the courage to stand under their own banner. I am not quarrelling with them. I am not a party to them, but they have the courage to stand up and say what they believe."

So even at that stage Sid showed respect for the Communist Party, and to me personally. I think it was unavoidable for him to differentiate between us and Militant Tendency. After all, about one quarter of the Executive Committee and dozens of branch and district council officers were members of the Communist Party and everyone recognised us as loyal and hard working members of the union.

In my defence of the Executive I said:

"...There was very little difference between us about the access outside bodies should have to the union. Unofficial circulars should not appear on the agenda at branch meetings... Branch Management Funds should not be used to distribute unofficial material or any other material other than that which had been authorised by the union."

Then I said:

"Now I come to the difficulty. If you are going to jump over it then you are going to put the union into trouble... How do you apply the rules of the union without infringing peoples' political, civil and democratic rights? If you are going to allow people to join a political party then that means that they must be able to distribute the literature of that organisation whether we like that organisation or not."

I then went on to deliver to the delegates what I still think was a learned lecture about a past event in our union's history – the Osborne Judgement – which for some years had a damaging effect on the union. I said:

"Osborne persecuted the union, and that went on for five or six years. At the end of the day and throughout the entire period, the union never took him to court and never took disciplinary action against him."

What I was saying was that I, and those who thought like me, were taking a sober decision to protect the union against possible litigation whereas Sid's impetuosity and bigotry would put it at risk. I think we were right. How could we take disciplinary action against a member who in his own time distributed a Militant or any other leaflet even if it was in opposition to our union policy?

I had no time for the Militant Tendency or the particular individuals involved. I think if they had had any guts they would have threatened Weighell with court action. They didn't. They expected us on the Executive to defend them, but when it came to the crunch they were nowhere to be seen. As it so happened one of the named individuals soon moved over and took a management job and another later served a term on the Executive Committee and acted throughout in a perfectly responsible manner. I got plenty of applause but was defeated by 54 votes to 23.

As late as the middle of 1982, we were still trying to get some rationality into our relations with Weighell. At that time the chairmanships of the various committees were due to be changed. In the normal course I would have become the chairman of the Negotiating Committee, the principal committee of the EC and the one with closest liaison with the General Secretary. Naturally, I would have very much liked to occupy that prestigious position before I retired altogether from the scene. But in the tense atmosphere that existed I thought something had to be done to bring about pacification in the leadership. Instead of accepting the chairmanship, I proposed Owen Conheeny, a former Merseyside councillor with impeccable Labour Party credentials that dated back further than Weighell's. Owen was reluctant. He was a sick man and regrettably died the following year. But he understood what I was trying to do and accepted the position. Ian Williams was anxious to be the secretary of that committee which would have made him the number two on the Executive. This would have been giving the very opposite signal from what most of us wanted. It would have been like waving a red rag to a bull for Ian had been implicated in the 'unofficial circulars' business and Weighell hated him with every tissue of his being. We had no difficulty squashing Ian's candidature and instead elected Jim Stevenson, a young Labour Party member with no connection with any Leftist groupings, as secretary. I had hoped that Weighell would have understood this significant gesture but by this time he was oblivious to anything but his own calculations.

I've just mentioned Ian Williams. His progression is interesting. He was the youngest member on the Executive, only 35 years of age and had been in the union only 10 years. He had received a better education than us oldies. He came from Liverpool and had often told us that he belonged to a 'soft left' group who were challenging Hatton and the Militant Tendency leadership who had control of Liverpool Council at that time. We took Ian at his word but we were a bit cautious of him for we thought he was too keen to talk to reporters who were always swarming around Unity House looking for information. In the end Sid overstretched himself and it led to his doom.

At the 1982 Labour Party Conference Sid voted for Tom Breakall the EEPTU nominee for the Labour Party Executive instead of for Alec Clark of the miners, contrary to the delegation's instructions. Our delegation consisted of only two EC members along with four national officers and 12 directly elected individual rank and file members who are in the Labour Party. He acted behind their back and was only found out by accident when there was a muddle in the counting of the votes. This double dealing was uncovered in the full glare of the television cameras. The delegates were furious. Their report to the Executive Committee said:

"At no time did the General Secretary consult with the delegation in regard to how the votes of the NUR were cast and we assumed the votes were cast according to the mandate... This delegation had no foreknowledge of the General Secretary's intention to deviate from instructions received..."

By now Sid had alienated almost everyone. The Executive Committee accepted his resignation unanimously. But Sid had one last throw that caused further divisions in the union. Along with his national officers he started a campaign to get a special conference of the union to ask him to withdraw his resignation. There was massive press and media backing. The London *Evening Standard* made that call in its entire front page under banner headlines 'Bring Back Weighell'. Frank Chapple waded in as well with an article in the *Mail on Sunday* entitled 'Why the Railwaymen Must Back Weighell'. But the membership had had enough. When the vote was declared I thought: how sad that a man of such talent should destroy himself! I hope I meet him sometime enjoying a peaceful evening's fishing. I'll give him the best fly from my fly-box then hasten back from the waterside as fast as my legs will carry me.

My first term on the Executive Committee coincided with the election of the Wilson Government of 1974. By the middle of the following year the wages and prices explosion was well under way. Civil Servants had won a 3% increase. The NUR was claiming 30%. When the Railway Tribunal awarded 27.5% after prolonged negotiations we made a decision to call a national railway strike. Immediately afterwards, Bill Edon who was our Southern District Council secretary and a party member, asked me to address a meeting he had arranged for the Guildford area. It was all young men who were in the audience with the exception of a grumpy-looking old boy in the front seat. I thought to myself; I'm going to have trouble with that old sour-puss. I knew that I had to set my stall to prevent him from influencing the young ones. When I rounded off with my peroration I thought I had done it quite well. Bill asked for questions. Dead silence. Bill then called for a vote endorsing the strike decision. Only one hand went up: old sour-puss. Bill was furious. He told these young men: "This is a democratic organisation. You voted for these people on the Executive Committee. They have taken the strike decision to protect your interests. It is your duty to support them." Then old sour-puss waded in. He was magnificent. By the time he was finished these young men must have been more frightened of him than I was at the beginning. Every hand went up to support the strike.

There was an interesting sequel to that meeting. That evening Bridget and I went to our hide-out that we had found in our cycling days. It was a caravan in a quiet little wooded dell between Guildford and Dorking. Next morning the old lady who owned the wood came to us in an agitated state: "Mr Nicolson, I've just had a phone call. The Prime Minister wants to see you urgently. You have to go back to London straight away." I don't know what she told the neighbours but when we went back on subsequent visits they gave us questioning looks.

This is what had happened. When Wilson heard about our strike decision he asked Weighell and Bowman to call on him. He told them that he would like to speak to the whole Executive Committee. The staff at Unity

House were on full alert. They operated like a military machine. EC members were scattered all over the country drumming up support for the strike. Everyone was reached. That afternoon EC members had an informal gathering at Unity House before making for Downing Street. We agreed that we would listen to Wilson but that no one would say a word in case something might come out that could be used against us.

My recollection of that meeting in the Cabinet Room is that of an array of ministers seated alongside the table with us on the other side. Wilson made the introductions but it was Denis Healey who did all the talking. He was very sombre. He spoke of the critical economic situation and the wages explosion. No one from the EC spoke – then old Jimmy Booth leaned forward and gave Healey such a roasting about the people at the bottom of the heap and the prices explosion. I can still see Healey throwing himself back in his chairs with eyes staring and lips down-turned. Jimmy had worked in the rail workshop in Glasgow and the rivet gun had made him deaf. He hadn't heard our earlier decision not to speak. But it did no harm. We got an extra two percent added to the pay offer and the strike was called off.

NUR membership was divided into four groups, all roughly the same size, and corresponding to similar sectors of the rail industry. Each group elected six members to the EC. The six from each group formed the four main sub-committees of the executive. I was elected by the goods and cartage members in the area, which stretched from the West Midlands to the South Coast. This membership was made up of workers in the big goods depots and the motor drivers who collected and delivered the traffic. Every matter concerning this group was put before the Goods and Cartage sub-committee, who made recommendations for endorsement or otherwise by the full EC. The bulk of my time, thought and energy was taken up by the affairs of this sub-committee. I had a column in our fortnightly newspaper *Transport Review*, where I reported on the decisions we had taken on all the main issues. I was the only EC member who did this on a regular basis.

The goods and cartage sector had declined rapidly since the end of the war from over 60,000 then to 20,000 when I went on to the EC in 1974. It was now no longer part of British Rail, having been hived-off by Labour's 1968 Transport Act, and given the title of National Carriers, and joined with the rest of nationalised road transport to form the umbrella organisation called the National Freight Corporation. This resulted in further rationalisation so that by 1980 the 100 large goods depots of war time had been reduced to 19 smaller ones. We had also about 2,500 National Carriers motor drivers working on contract to British Rail parcels service. Then in 1981 at one stroke they were all made redundant when BR closed down their main parcels operations.

It is not difficult to see that this was not an easy time for EC members, and especially for those of us responsible for the goods and cartage sector. The members on the job were disgruntled. Their representatives at depot level had once been generals with an army behind them and able to deal with grievances by their own strength. Now they were lance-corporals with no power. They were embittered, and some of them tended to divert their frustration against us in the union leadership.

Redundancies were the biggest problem. We made a lot of noise about this with BR and National Carriers, but the job losses continued. However, we did get in the end agreement that redundant National Carrier employees would get priority for vacancies on BR. I don't know of a single person who failed to be accommodated in this way. I have in front of me, my last article in *Transport Review*. Under the headline 'Without the union it would have been much worse', I said:

"...The union has saved everything that could be saved... alternative jobs were made available on BR for those who wanted them...
In 1981... on NCL average earnings increased for that year by 17%... We did better for our Freightliner members... In 1981 we negotiated the highest rate in road haulage for them... in 1982... we kept our members in the top pay bracket."

I concluded:

"Without the union things would have been a hundred times worse... It is as if there are lean years and fat years; periods of defence and periods of advance. But you cannot create a union overnight. You build in difficult times so that you can take advantage of the situation when it improves."

One of the most difficult issues I had to face in my last years on the EC concerned the privatisation of the National Freight Corporation. About this I felt I had a special responsibility having been elected by our members in that company. This was the first big undertaking to be privatised by the Thatcher Government. It was a new and rather startling experience for us, for it must be remembered that the majority of workers – and the union leadership too – had only known the environment of a nationalised industry.

At first the Government intended to sell it off in shares as a normal kind of private company. But this became an unlikely proposition when the NFC lost its biggest contract and its fortunes looked very bleak indeed. It was at this moment that some on the top management of NFC showed themselves to be far-seeing entrepreneurs and jumped in with the idea of a management / employee buy-out. Eventually this became a reality and

NFC changed hands in February 1982. It was not a co-operative. It was described as a management-led consortium. In reality it was a private firm in which a majority of employees and pensioners owned on average around a couple of hundred pounds of shares, purchased in most cases via a loan from the bank and arranged by NFC management. Our problem in the union was how we should respond to this, for us, strange new situation. I drafted the report and after some discussion it was adopted by a majority on the EC. Here is part of it:

"(We) welcomed this initiative as the only option to keep the company intact. The union has also repeatedly declared its opposition to denationalisation; and a fundamental part of union policy is the extension of public ownership of transport by the next Labour Government... We feel, therefore, that members who purchase shares in the consortium should be safeguarded in any future Labour Government legislation...
We feel that it is also necessary to clarify the union's position in relation to members who purchase shares in the consortium. It should be made clear that this is purely and solely a matter for the individual concerned and, apart from the recommendation made above, the union accepts no responsibility in this connection. The union represents its members as employees and not as shareholders, and no advice or services can be provided in connection with shareholding..."

Although we were terribly apprehensive about this move to the private sector, I still think we adopted a sober and realistic attitude in welcoming the initiative of management. I am sure it helped to safeguard the jobs of many of our members at that uncertain time. We also succeeded in getting the new company to underwrite the travel concessions and pensions rights of its former BR employees, who now had no connection whatever with the railways. I am in this category. How I appreciate it when I collect my free passes for Lands End or John o' Groats!

At the same time the report reflects how strongly influenced we were by labour movement ideas about the superiority of traditional forms of nationalisation as we had known them in the coal mines and railways. Two years after my retirement when I became a student for the first time in my life I did a project on NFC privatisation.

Here is one of my conclusions:

Privatisation: How to cope with it

It is time now to attempt to draw some conclusions from this study. The TUC and practically every union in the country are today engaged in campaigns to defend the nationalised industries and public services from privatisation. There is a fundamentalist socialist position in this. It is that nationalisation dispossessed capitalist ownership thereby eliminating their source of economic and political power, and privatisation will reverse that process. Indeed, Conservative spokesmen speak about a 'people's capital market' which will transform the class structure of our society by creating millions of worker-shareholders. In these days of the giant multi-national corporation and polarisation of wealth it is difficult to take that seriously. Will their £700 share-holdings change the political and trade union allegiance of the workers in the NFC? The study did not produce any evidence to that effect. Shareholdings were regarded as savings. Socialists in the unions can turn this to their advantage. The 1982 TUC-LP policy document 'Economic Planning and Industrial Democracy' indicates that a major aim of a future Labour Government will be to step up investment – private as well as public – in industry. One proposal is that pension funds should be guided in this direction.

And if pensions, which are a form of savings, why not workers' shares which are another form of savings? It should not be too difficult to get Labour to adapt its policy to regard workers' shares in the same light as building society investments, and with similar guarantees and protection. Among other things, this would neutralise opposition to renationalisation.

It would not be honest to finish on this subject without mentioning that £100 share purchased at the time of privatisation (1981) is now worth £13,000 (January 1992), so there are a few thousand NFC employees and pensioners who have done very well out of that privatisation. I wouldn't say that will always be the case.

The NFC was the first large undertaking to be privatised by the Thatcher Government. They were desperate to help it on its way. It was sold for a song. In the end the Government only received £5million from the sale. The NFC privatisation got off to a very good start. Apart from anything else they took over a large number of sites in town centres that they didn't need and soon sold them off. With all these advantages they could hardly go wrong. As for myself I did not benefit by one penny from that bonanza. I refused to take up any shares, although I believe had I made the right responses I might have been given a wad of them for nothing. Being a well-known NUR Executive Committee member at the centre of the controversy this would have been a very welcome boost for the purchase of shares by employees at the beginning stage when management was not certain how it would catch on. I considered anything of that kind would have been unethical.

Chapter 10 - Off the Rails

I was due to retire from the Executive Committee (EC) at the end of 1982. In the middle of that year a decision had been taken to close Camden depot, which had been my official workplace since coming to London in 1950. By that time there were only about a couple of dozen men employed there. It didn't even have a manager, but was reduced to the status of a sub-depot of Paddington whose manager, Lloyd Williams, was also responsible for Camden. I had met Lloyd about 10 years earlier when he was in charge of the Bristol depot. He was a mate of Jack King who was on the Executive at that time. Unlike any other manager I have known Lloyd was, and remained, a member of the NUR He had a rather aggressive personality and had been abusive to one of our Camden motor drivers. When Johnny Cotier our NUR branch secretary, threatened to take this up with his superiors he used his NUR membership to get the thing squashed.

In line with the understanding between National Carriers and the NUR, everyone at Camden had the option either to transfer to King's Cross depot or take redundancy pay. As I was on the EC, I had my choice to go to Kings Cross confirmed by letter. Then on January 5th 1983 when I turned up there in working clothes all ready to start work I was told by Lloyd, who was now manager there, that there was no job for me. He explained, with a hint of malice in his voice, that the letter confirming my appointment was no longer valid as there had been a re-organisation of the company, which had eliminated the authority in whose name it had been issued. I must confess this knocked the stuffing out of me. The previous week I had been negotiating with the people at the top and now here I was being cut down to size.

I immediately contacted Jimmie Knapp, then the NUR divisional officer of the NUR responsible for dealing with individual's cases with National Carriers. I'm sure that if I had persisted Jimmie would have succeeded in getting me the position at King's Cross. But strangely, higher management straight away offered me double redundancy pay to resolve the matter. My reaction was mixed. If I insisted in taking up the job it might end up in pushing out one of my old Camden mates. Besides, I was only a couple of years off pension age. I also realised that my role in the union could only be that of an old 'has-been'. Nevertheless, I was very sad when I signed the document that my days with National Carriers were over.

I am still not sure who was behind that coup; whether it was Lloyd settling some old score that I had forgotten about, or whether it was someone higher up the ladder. But that was eight years ago. Now, for the past couple of years I've again become linked with Lloyd. This time we are allies not antagonists. We exchange the courtesy of a handshake but don't talk about the past. Our alliance is against the management of the Pensions Fund. For some years now they have used the surplus in the Fund to avoid making a Company contribution. We argue that part of that surplus should go to the pensioners.

Due to the good offices of Len Bound, another NUR divisional officer, I soon had a job at West Hampstead rail station. The work consisted of keeping the place clean and issuing and checking that passengers had valid tickets. This was the first time in my working life that I was in direct contact with the public – if we discount my four years as a party organiser. Obviously, this kind of relationship with a cross-section of people is bound to have some influence in your outlook and psychology over a period of time. There was only one railwayman on the station each shift, but as the work was light compared with what I had been accustomed to, it was no great hardship to help young mums up the very steep stairs with their prams, especially as most of them were quite attractive. Nevertheless, I was quite amused and a little moved, when I noticed a commendation to me in the staff newspaper. Apparently letters had been sent in expressing appreciation for my helpful attitude to passengers.

Regrettably, there is usually another side to everyday life. There was a young girl, probably around 17 years of age, who frequently avoided paying her fare. She would wait till there was a crowd at the barrier then rush through. It was so obvious what she was up to. She did the same at the start of her journey and I would get a phone call to watch out for her. I did get a hold of her a number of times and warned her that she was being watched and would sooner or later come to grief. Her response was to bring a mob of tough-looking boyfriends some nights to see her off. I took this to be something of a warning to me and when I closed the station at 11 at night I always had an iron bar hidden up my sleeve. The inevitable happened and one morning the railway police nabbed her.

That girl and her boy friends were pretty unpleasant customers. Still, the incident upset me a lot. She was a trainee hairdresser and I'm sure got very little pay. Often she must have been in the position where she simply didn't have the £2 fare. Of course, if she had been strong enough willed and stopped buying the gum that was a-champing her jaws, and given up smoking, and gone straight home every night instead of playing around with a mob of skinheads, she could have passed through the ticket barrier with head held high and dropped a valid ticket in my outstretched hand. Isn't that a heavy penance for any 17-year-old? Anyway, the opportunity

arose for me to move to the dispatch office at Euston. I was thereby re-
lieved of pondering over this insoluble problem of everyday life.

The Euston job didn't last long. There was another rail reorganisation
and my post, along with another hundred or so, moved to Birmingham. It
looked as though I was moving into the league where you boasted not
about the number of pints you could put away but the number of redundancies you had swallowed. I decided I had done enough work for a
lifetime, at least the paid kind. I intended to do the unpaid kind and give
the remainder of my time to party activity.

I felt that with my experience in the trade unions the most effective contribution I could give the party was to help Pete Carter in the industrial
department. I had noticed an advertisement about a course on Trade
Union Studies at Middlesex Polytechnic. It sounded interesting and fitted
into what I wanted to do. I applied without expecting too much and was
quite excited when I learned that I had been accepted as a mature student
for the one-year full-time course. It was practically half a century since I
had left school and that schooling could hardly be described as study. But
I had read quite a lot, if only over a limited range of subjects directly
related to my interests in the labour movement, and had engaged in some
self-study if preparing for meetings and taking the occasional class can be
so described. But to become a student at my age was quite a leap.

I can say in defence of those at the Polytechnic who had the courage to
choose me, an oldie, that I have never worked harder in all my life. I
burned the midnight oil. I rarely lifted my head from a book. At the end
of each day I was totally exhausted. It was an intensive course. It included
six separate subjects: trade-union law, history, politics, sociology, economics, and for the poorly educated ones like myself, English. The tutors
were very patient.

What did I learn? I got a glimpse at the basics of some subjects that were
totally new to me, and in that sense widened my general knowledge. But I
think the most important thing is that it compelled me to look at points of
view that were different from my own, instead of dismissing them out of
hand. I think if I had had that schooling much earlier in my life I would
have been more cautious, more circumspect in arriving at conclusions
rather than jumping to them as so often was the case. I also came to have
greater respect for scholars. I don't mean people who show off by quoting
lots of sources, but only those who are not afraid to think new thoughts
and express them simply. Now, even when reading a newspaper, I think I
can recognise the reporter who tries to see under the surface and the one
who only states the obvious.

The students on my course were a varied bunch. There were a few – male
and female – that already had some experience in the trade-union move-

movement and wanted to improve their effectiveness, or perhaps even become trade union officers. There one or two Young Socialists straight from school whom one could almost see as the future careerists. But the largest segment – reflecting the positive discrimination policies of the Polytechnic – were young women, some of whom gradually coalesced into a fairly stable group who described themselves as radical feminists. I found most of them insensitive and intolerant.

I know what I have just said will stir up a hornets' nest, especially as I am referring to my personal reaction and cannot present hard evidence or establish proof. Sometimes what I am objecting to expresses itself in the concept that 'Man is the enemy of woman', not capitalism or the social system. There are subtle variations of the theme, but in the end they give an imbalance to our movement. I think this was the case with our party paper 7 Days. But that did not stop me from having a regular round every week and selling it at Unity House and ASLEF headquarters. I am also very conscious that I so often use the term 'rail man' and not 'rail woman'. That reflects the actual working environment that I have known. I know more women work on the railways now than an ever before, but that never applied to the sector where I was employed. I totally reject the suggestion that this has made me a male chauvinist. I can quote by the yard the women in the movement whose ability and dedication I have always recognised, and the many I still have contact with to this day.

I think of my actual experience in the NUR during one of my periods on the Executive Committee we had the one and only woman up till now to serve at that level. I doubt if anyone would want to claim that she made any distinctive contribution to the membership, male or female, and when her term was up she left the industry and the union. At the same time I know many women members who play a leading role at branch and district level. The fact that they have not gone higher is not due to male prejudice in the union but to their role as mothers, and the current division of labour, which in many cases puts the bulk of the work in the home on their shoulders. So let us continue to campaign for the positive measures that will make it possible for women to be elected to the top positions – but on merit – and not sink to posing female chauvinism against male chauvinism.

The 1970s was a period of trade union growth and self-confidence, but the decade ended in the 'winter of discontent' with the unions and the Labour Government in sharp conflict. It has become customary for the left, and especially the trade union left, to blame the Wilson and Callaghan Governments for taking a tough line against what was our favourite slogan at that time, 'free collective bargaining'. Since then I have continued to wonder whether it wasn't that we in the Communist Party were taking up an ultra-leftist line.

I think one of the processes that had started a bit earlier was a turn by the Communist Party away from general political campaigning to concentrating on work in the trade unions. My own personal role confirms this. I had been a parliamentary and local government candidate throughout the 50s, but our votes continued to fall steadily. It seemed a waste of effort to continue to work in this field, especially for members like myself who had some foothold in the union. I ceased to be a candidate and concentrated all my energy into the union and industrial arena. This was a general trend and is proved by the scaling down of communist election work in the whole of the country at that time.

Here is another example of the political consequence of the 'turn to industry'. When John Mahon retired as secretary of the London District Committee of the party, it was Frank Stanley and not Sam Aaronovitch who took over that position. Frank was a highly respected shop steward convenor but I'm sure he did not have anything like the political acumen of Sam. The factory proletariat had been elevated above the political thinker. A corresponding development was the increasingly dominating role of the industrial department in the leadership of the party. This became especially the case with such a strong personality as Bert Ramelson in charge of that department.

In the early part of the 80s I was still of the opinion that the Thatcher Government would sooner or later be brought down by trade union action. I think this was a view quite widely held at the time. In the NUR, for example, Sid Weighell took the initiative in forming a triple alliance of the NUR, the miners and the steelworkers. I am not saying he had any thought about bringing the Government to its knees, but he must have had in mind that industrial power would be an effective defence against Thatcher's attacks.

By the middle of the 80s, this was a view that was difficult to sustain. Thatcher had already brought in a train of restrictive anti-union measures. The miners' strike had been defeated and the NUM was split in two and weaker than it had ever been. But even more important, widespread unemployment had resulted in a slump in union membership. The entire labour movement, trade unions, Labour Party and the Communist Party began a process of rethinking. This led to very bad-tempered bickering inside our party by those who still thought in terms of the primacy of trade-union struggle.

In a letter to *Marxism Today* I expressed my thoughts:

"Congratulations to MT for the John Edmonds interview. Edmonds is very honest when he says: "That within the next decade trade unions are not going to be in the position to force contract cleaners, for exam-

ple, to pay reasonable pay and conditions through trade union organi-
sation".

His conclusion is that Governmental action will be needed. The trade
union role is supplementary.

"One could go much further and say that the same is true in tradition-
ally highly organised sectors. Miners, for example, will not prosper very
much in the future on the basis of industrial militancy alone. The future
depends on the kind of fuel policy adopted by the government of the day.
The same applies on the railways. The rail unions have tried every
possible permutation of industrial action to defend jobs but with very
little success. Recent discussions between the Labour leaders and the
Rail Board about creating more jobs in the industry are the first glim-
mer of hope for decades."

Peter Hain, in his book *Political Strikes* took up a similar theme. In a
review of the book for *7 Days* I wrote:

"Hain says calls for a general strike by some on the left... were at best
token and desperate ones, and at worst cynical attempts to 'expose' union
and Labour Party leaders, who as everyone knew, simply could not deliver a general strike even if they had wanted to." (p 236)

I think that is being very gentle with that particular brand of Left-
adventurism. Hain's final chapter 'A New Unionism' is the one that is
most likely to encounter a grinding of teeth and mutterings from some
trade union Lefts.

"The traditional insistence on the primacy of the industrial struggle in
the workplace, rather than the broader class struggle with other social
movements, has contributed to this one dimensional trade unionism"
(p312).

"His final conclusion comes very close to Pete Carter's recent report to
the Communist Party Executive Committee."

I have already mentioned that 'new thinking' led to bad-tempered bickering inside the Communist Party. In a review for *7 Days* of a pamphlet
'Consensus or Socialism' by Bert Ramelson, I wrote:

"This pamphlet is the write-up of the Ralph Fox memorial lecture delivered by Bert Ramelson in November, 1986. Its main thrust is directed
against the Kinnock-Hattersley leadership of the Labour Party and the
revisionist leadership of the Communist Party and Marxism Today. Ramelson argues that Kinnock and Hattersley are pursuing the same
strategy as Gaitskell and Wilson, which was aimed at winning the middle

ground. That policy, he says, led to disillusionment and the progressive alienation of the working class and labour voter. Against this, Ramelson poses the fundamentalist line of the Communist Campaign Group: 'There is only one way out of the dilemma... that is socialism and the intensification of the class struggle'."

"Ramelson's status in our movement is associated with his former position as national industrial organiser of the CP and his views on industry and the unions carry some weight. He blames "Kinnock, the majority of the TUC council and the Communist Party" for failure to mobilise solidarity behind the miners and print workers. Many will find these charges deeply wounding. Take the print strike where he and those who think like him had their greatest influence. Neither Sogat nor the NGA were able to get their members outside London to take strike action in support of their News International colleagues. Ron Todd and the TGWU executive instructed their T.N.T. lorry drivers not to cross picket lines, but without success. (Only the NUR delivered solidarity). In the face of this almost total refusal of those closest to the dispute to take supporting action it is sheer escapism to put the blame on Kinnock, Willis or Carter."

Another issue of the 80s which caused much controversy inside the Communist Party and on the left generally was the Common Market. I think opposition in the early days was based on our optimism that we were more likely to have a left Labour Government in Britain that would move in the direction of socialism and we did not want to be held back by conservative European institutions. I recall that shortly after Sid Weighell became general secretary of the NUR he arranged for Tony Benn and Shirley Williams to put their opposing views on the Common Market to our Executive Committee. A majority were on Benn's side against the Market.

By the middle of the 80s positions were being reversed. The Tories under Thatcher were showing increasing hostility to the idea of the European Social Charter, and we on the left after two Labour General Election defeats, were less confident about rapid social advance. I had been working (in a voluntary unpaid capacity) with Pete Carter in the party's industrial department and had prepared a paper on the European Community. I think it is interesting from a number of angles. It expresses my view about the limitation of purely trade union action and the need for a much broader form of political movement. I don't know whether my yearning for something like the Peoples' Charter Movement of last century was political romanticism, but now on the eve of a general election I am quite certain that popular support for the idea of the European Social Charter will be an important factor in Labour's favour. Here are some extracts from my paper:

"This article is an attempt to present some ideas about the kind of overall Trade Union strategy that the Left should be thinking about in connection with the Single European Market of 1992. Most sections of the Left now accept that the European Economic Community is here to stay and there is no alternative but to work within it to get the best possible deal for British workers... What we are concerned with is a trade union strategy that matches the scenario as far ahead as one can see at the present time..."

" ...The European T.U.C. and also socialist and communist M.E.P's and some other groups within the European Parliament are pressing for the adoption of a Charter of Workers' Rights that would apply throughout the whole Community. Broadly, the aim is that there should be upward harmonisation of employee's rights and social benefits throughout the E.EC As everyone knows, the Thatcher Government is the fiercest opponent of this social dimension..."

"However, a number of things need to be said about activities at the European level by Trade Unions, political parties or governments. They will involve only a handful of officials and are therefore removed from ordinary workers..."

"Nor should one expect too much too soon from cross-frontier trade union solidarity, though in some cases a common policy and joint action will be needed right from the beginning. This applies, for example, on the railways where we will have French and British rail workers jointly operating the Channel Tunnel rail link..."

"... It will be useful to look at a recent study into the likely impact of 1992 on the West Midlands. This shows that between 1978/86 one third of manufacturing jobs – 300,000 – had been lost and the pressure for further job cuts at Rover and large private manufacturing firms continued. At the same time the new jobs created in service industries and assembly were resulting in a massive low pay problem: 43% of workers in this once very prosperous region now earn pay that is below the Council of Europe's 'decency level'. Many of these workers are unskilled males, ethnic minorities and women part-time workers; some are working in small sweat shops or even at home, or are employed by small fly-by-night private contractors. This Hong Kongisation applies to many regions in Britain and to inner-cities. It is a process that is accelerating everywhere and the reality is that the workers involved do not have – and never will have – any real bargaining power that can be made effective by traditional union methods such as strikes or other forms of industrial action.

"How can these groups of workers... gain from the European Community? If not by industrial action then it must be through political action in its broadest meaning... We have to think of a fairly loose movement rather than an organisation based on the rigid structures of trade unions though they must be linked to the unions. And because they have little or no industrial power, their activities would be a mix of community work, legal test cases and mass demonstrations..."

"How exciting to think back 100 years to the great revival that New Unionism brought into being; or go back a further 50 years to the Peoples' Charter Movement – the greatest mass movement of ordinary people that this country has ever known. In both these cases workers recognised the need for political action to get the legal framework that would give them protection at work and better social conditions, for at that stage they also lacked industrial muscle..."

We are now in 1992 and one thing that is becoming clear is that Britain is at the bottom end of the European Social Charter. I know we are nowhere near building anything like the great Peoples' Charter Movement that swept the country a century and a half ago. But an increasing number of unions are now broadening their activities to go beyond purely workshop issues. My own union, now called Rail, Maritime and Transport since the amalgamation with the National Union of Seamen, has set up retired members sections. For the past year I have been the President of one of them. We are at present conducting a vigorous campaign on pensions. Our immediate target is the N.F.C. Pensions Fund management who we feel have been very unfair to retired members of their occupational pension schemes.

The N.F.C. Pensions Fund had accumulated a large surplus, and apparently the law lays it down that the Fund surplus must not go beyond a certain level. I suppose the reason for this is to prevent Fund managers from limiting current pensions so that they can increase them at a later date when they themselves are due to retire. Anyway, the obvious way to reduce the surplus would be to increase existing pensions, especially as it was past contributions that laid the basis for the surplus. But N.F.C. Fund managers decided otherwise. For the past three years they have solved the problem by what they call a 'contributions holiday'. For three months in the past three years neither the company nor employees have been required to pay any contributions into the Fund. For both these parties this is a very substantial benefit. For the employees it is equivalent to a pay increase – perhaps this is part of management's calculation aimed at keeping the workers from pressing for too much in the annual pay round; for the company it amounts to a very large boost to their profits. I feel indignant about this. To me it is an act of piracy. Pension funds were brought into being to provide pensions for retired workers yet they are the ones who do not benefit from the surplus in the Fund.

For these past three years Lloyd Williams (I referred to him earlier. He was the manager at King's Cross who 'sacked' me when I came off the

NUR Executive Committee) and I have been kicking up an almighty row at the annual meeting of N.F.C. pensioners. It took us some time to realise the injustice of what was being done and a little longer for other pensioners to catch on to what we were saying. At the last meeting we won a unanimous demand for a fairer method of distributing the surplus. From this year we will have a directly elected pensioner's representative on the Fund Committee. I am not sure that will make much difference unless the representative has access to independent professional advice.

I say that because Pension Fund matters are very complex for a layman. When I was on the NUR Executive I sometimes attended Pension Fund meetings as an observer, the actual 'negotiations' being conducted by a national officer who had been briefed by our own office staff who specialised on pensions matters. I am not ashamed to confess that much of the time I was out of my depth. I don't think that was because I am particularly dumb. We have been reading a lot in the newspapers recently about the strange goings-on in the Daily Mirror Pension Fund, so obviously I am not the only one who didn't grasp in time what the professionals were up to. I am sure a lot more is going to be revealed as the Mirror case proceeds. I only hope that the unions especially will take advantage of the interest this will arouse to find a more effective way of monitoring the affairs of pension funds.

I think a much bigger ethical question arises. I have absolutely no doubt that the managers of the N.F.C. Funds are decent honourable men. How then could they act in the way they did? It really puzzles me. Is it that once people reach their level in the business world they become so imbued with the idea of maximising profits that there is little place in their outlook for humanitarian considerations?

The 80's was also the decade when the Communist Party of Great Britain began to break apart. The first break-away was led by Sid French, the Surrey district secretary. It was a club of fanatics who were still living in the atmosphere of the Bolshevik insurrection. They were so out of date that nobody took them seriously. It was better that they were no longer in the C.P.G.B. The last thing I saw in one of their publications was a description of Gorbachev as the Eric Hammond of the communist movement. Then there was the Communist Campaign Group, which later formed the Communist Party of Britain. This was a more serious split as they won control of the _Morning Star_ they also took with them a number of leading trade union activists.

The loss of the _Morning Star_ was a very sad blow to Bridget and myself, as it was to a very large part of our remaining members. It had been our flagship for half a century. Both of us had given a good part of our life to keeping the paper alive. Bridget, and her colleagues in this part of North London, must have raised tens of thousands of £'s for the Fighting Fund.

While I worked at Camden Goods depot I had a regular daily sale. I once timed myself: it took two hours of my eight hours working day just to travel between the different locations where I had readers. And on Saturday mornings after I had done my four hours work stint, I sold the paper for another couple of hours at Camden Town market, and Bridget would be doing the same at Swiss Cottage tube station.

Our own CPGB held a Special Congress towards the end of 1991 where a new constitution was adopted and the party renamed 'Democratic Left'. This was the first congress in my 50 years membership in which I was not fully involved. I have registered my membership in this new party but so far have not taken part in any activity. My reasoning tells me that this political change is correct, but every tissue in my being is so steeped in past doctrine that the old frame is not capable of making such a fast turn.

All my life I have been an activist not a political thinker. The great ideological upheavals in the international communist movement left me comparatively untouched. I found Khrushchev's secret speech denouncing Stalin interesting, but it certainly did not shake my feeling for the Soviet Union. I suppose I continued to think of Stalin, in spite of the terrible revelations, as a great historical figure who had moved human society forward. How I rejoiced when Khrushchev told the Americans that the USSR would overtake them in living standards by 1970.

Then, when most of our party were at each other's throats about Soviet intervention in Hungary in 1956 all my thoughts were concentrated on St. Pancras Borough Council elections where I was a Communist candidate. Some years later when Soviet troops went into Czechoslovakia I was on their side. I know Dubcek's clarion call was for socialism with a human face. But how could the Czech's claim greater ideological purity or political experience than the tried and tested leadership of the Soviet Union? I think that was the extent of my reasoning.

When Gorbachev became leader of the Soviet Communist Party I felt all my faith in the Soviet party had been confirmed. Of course there were blemishes on real existing socialism. How could such a transformation of human society be achieved without scars? But the stage had come when these would be healed. And the initiative for change had come from forces from within the party. Didn't this prove the dynamism of Bolshevik ideology and organisation? Now, Soviet socialism would again become a great attractive force for socialism throughout the world. That is how I thought about things for the first five years of Gorbachev's leadership. I was not alone. Wasn't there renewed excitement everywhere, which went far beyond the ranks of Communist parties and new hopes for peace and social advance?

Then, in the past year everything in the socialist world seems to have gone wrong. In Yugoslavia there is war between the republics. People who yesterday addressed each other as 'Comrade' have turned mortal enemies and are engaged in murder. The great centralised Soviet state has collapsed like a house of cards. Nationalism, not internationalism, is the driving force for millions of people. Ethnic tensions are rising. In Georgia there is something approaching civil war. In the streets of Moscow and St. Petersburg near anarchy prevails. Nobody knows when the explosion will take place but everyone is expecting it. Gorbachev is reviled while former Politburo colleagues cannot run fast enough to embrace capitalism. The masses of ordinary people are shouting their heads off for the goodies of the West but don't want to hear the social costs they will have to pay for them. The magic they have been given is the 'Free Market' and the ending of price and rent control. Who can predict what will happen? That is the depressing view as I write this on 3/1/1992.

In the past year it is as though I have gone through a hundred bereavements. Every day saw a new setback to the hopes and beliefs I held most dear. The Communist Party of the Soviet Union was my party; for me the Communist Party of Great Britain was still a section of the international Communist Movement within which the CPSU played the leading role. The Soviet Union was my country not Britain, not even Scotland- now it no longer exists. I have given all my life to Communism. Now, we are told it is dead.

A few days ago I read two letters. One was from Kate Hudson, who up until our special congress in November was secretary of our London district committee. She couldn't accept the majority decision of the congress and wrote to say that she and a number of others would continue to call themselves Communists. The other letter was from Bill Shepherd; he had been a party activist up until the split in 1984, and for many years was secretary of the largest NUR branch in the country. Bill wrote about Communism: "I was wrong, wrong, wrong... " I understand and sympathise with both of them. But now we must use the head as well as the heart.

Yes, for me, and for millions of Communists throughout the world, the collapse of the Communist Party of the Soviet Union was a shattering blow. It has affected me physically and mentally. I now suffer from chronic depression. Is everything that I lived and worked for only a mirage? Why was I so blind to what so many people were saying about the CPSU? How could I have been wrong for so long?

What does all this self-questioning signify? It shows that I am still perplexed and bewildered. I am uncertain and nervous about everything. I often think what is the purpose of life if the raison d'être has disappeared.

My personality is changed. I am touchy and irritable. This has made relations difficult with some who are very dear to me.

I am trying to get out of this morbid state. I am trying to understand what has really happened in the Soviet Union. In the last few days I have read the latest books of Yeltsin, Shevardnadze and Gorbachev's 'The August Coup'. Here is what Gorbachev says:

"Thirty-two of the seventy-two secretaries of regional party committees in the Russian Federation declared that Gorbachev should be called to account..." (p 13)

"For a long time I really did think that the CPSU could be reformed. But the August coup destroyed these hopes... Many party committees decided to help the plotters... the coup wiped out any hope of reforming the CPSU... That is why I resigned the post of General Secretary and proposed that the Central Committee should dissolve itself..." (p 46)

"Among the collection of critics and oppositionists there are also Communist fundamentalists who are incapable of freeing themselves from the grip of dogmatist ideas..." (p 112)

So there is absolutely no doubt the CPSU is moribund. And the accusations about it being bureaucratic and reactionary were correct. Yet for so long I angrily rejected these charges. And that reference of Gorbachev about 'Communist fundamentalists' and 'dogmatist ideas' I take very much to heart. Still, Gorbachev, in spite of all he has experienced, remains a socialist. He says:

"In discussing socialism we must recognise it was the model of socialism that we had in our country which proved a failure, and not the socialist idea itself..."

But what model of socialism has Gorbachev now got in mind?

"We must remove all the obstacles and impediments ... in the path to a market economy... offer complete freedom to business... and speed up the creation of the main institutions of a market economy." (p 44)

I am slowly coming to accept that the Soviet model of socialism, which I had looked up to all my life, has gone for ever. But I am still finding some difficulty in completely embracing Gorbachev's new vision of a market economy type of socialism. It does not appear to be much different from Neil Kinnock's version and as communists we used to condemn that as 'reformism', not socialism but simply an attempt to modify the worst evils of capitalism.

There are many on the left, far outside the Communist Party, who also have serious doubts about market economy socialism. Not so long ago this controversy was at the centre of one of the fiercest struggles in Labour's history and nearly rent the Party apart. It started with Gaitskell's attempt to remove clause 4 of the Labour Party constitution, and ended up in the break-away led by David Owen, Shirley Williams and William Rodgers. It is true that the Social Democrats have disappeared from the British political scene, but hasn't the present leadership of the Labour Party taken up much of their ideology?

I can understand the new people who have come to power in the shambles of the command economy. I wonder if that enthusiasm is due to the fact that they have never experienced a free-market environment. I noticed in the newspapers the other day that free market euphoria is already beginning to wane in Poland and a new government committed to slowing down that process has been appointed.

If we look at the more successful market economies – the United States of America or the European Community – life is not all that wonderful for a very big segment of the population in these countries. They suffer serious deprivation all their life. Here in Britain, on the eve of a General Election, government leaders appear on television every day, obviously bewildered and uncertain about what is happening in the market place. It is clear that they have no control over it and the so-called self-regulating mechanisms are not working; least of all for the millions who have lost their jobs, and many of them their homes as well. I think back to the same kind of despair of my own youth: the slump lasted from 1924 to 1938. That was the situation in most capitalist countries. It took preparations for a world war to get the economy moving again. So even if the Soviet experiment has failed I'm not going to be too quick in singing the praises of capitalism. How could I after reading yesterday that Lanarkshire's Ravenscraig, the last remaining steelworks in Scotland, is to be closed down?

I think about other experiments to construct a more humane economy. There was Robert Owens's factory reform at New Lanark 150 years ago. Owens's dreams were never realised but his effort inspired later generations to continue the search. I also think of the Co-operative movement. I've already mentioned that in my own childhood the Co-op stores were an essential part of our life. That was where all the basic things for living came from. Now newer and trendier forms of trading have very largely surpassed the Co-ops.

When I am in a gloomy mood about my failed utopias I try and gain some comfort from a book I read some years ago. It was H.G. Wells' _History of the World_. This planet of ours has existed for hundreds of millions of years. Great civilisations have appeared and disappeared, but human progress continues. Looked at in this light, the 70 years of Soviet social-ism is but a blink of the eye. What appears to me from my own short life span as a tragedy is nothing in terms of human history. I'm sure the search for a humane socialism will continue.

There is no denying that dreams are a part of living. That dreams have magical powers has been known throughout history. In early times they have been interpreted by the sages to inspire heroic deeds. They have also been used as a narcotic to ease the pain of disappointments and defeats. I used to have all kinds of dreams but they are denied me in my old age. Now I have reached the stage when I have to look back on my life and ask: has it been worthwhile or has it been wasted?

I have no reason to doubt that if I had not followed the path that I did I would have grown up very similar to my childhood contemporaries. I would have found work on the railways or the steelworks, married some-one with a similar background to my own, had a family, enjoyed a few pints during the week, and at weekends fished for trout in the Clyde. I'm not denigrating that lifestyle. Mr. and Mrs. Average have nothing to apologise for. By doing their everyday work and living in a neighbourly way they are making their contribution to society.

I am different. That is not said as a boast. I am trying to size myself up. I think being a communist activist has given me a much richer life and made me a better person than I would have been had I not taken that path. For one thing, life has been exciting. I think of all the campaigns I have been involved in: strikes, demonstrations, electioneering; exhaust-ing yes but never dull. Then there is the self-assurance I gained: able to stand up to the fiercest heckling at the hustings, or full of confidence at the negotiating table opposite the toughest management. It amuses me to look back and see myself as a child: shy and retiring. Who would have imagined then that he would turn out something of an agitator?

I think also of the much richer intellectual life I have had through my marriage to Bridget and my association with so many other educated people I have come across in the party. Just by working with them I learned how to study and delved into areas of knowledge that would otherwise have been closed to me. I am sure that sixty years ago no teacher at Woodside School thought that that miserable little fellow sit-ting in the front row would ever be able to string a sentence together, and here he is writing his autobiography!

I am sure that I have made a fair contribution to my fellow workers and to society, sometimes as an individual and often as part of a collective. On the railway depot it would be by winning a penny here and a penny there on tonnage rates. As a union representative at national level it would be by helping to make work and retirement better than before. As a local government and parliamentary candidate I helped to keep alive the movement for better housing, health and welfare facilities. I also gave much time and energy to campaigns for a world at peace. I don't think my life has been useless.

I believe I am a better person. In Britain no one joined the Communist Party for purposes of self-advancement or enrichments. On the contrary, it was more likely to lead to persecution and financial hardship. You had to force yourself to do things that were difficult and demanding. Most of the time you were swimming against the stream. To keep that up for a lifetime is some achievement. It needed strength and character. I think my life as a communist has given me some of that quality. So even though I no longer dream but look at myself in the cold harsh light of reality I have no regrets: my life has not been wasted.

I said earlier that with the break up of the Communist Party I had not been involved in public campaigning for the past couple of years. I should modify that statement. I have already talked about being President of the Union's Retired Members Section for the London Midland district. The other area of activity was the campaign against the Poll Tax. In our locality this was something of a spontaneous development. I can't remember how it began. It was not initiated by any one political organisation. It included Left Labour Councillors and activists, Socialist Party members, a few Communists, as well as quite a number of young men and women who kept their particular brand of politics to themselves. We engaged in the usual kinds of activities: leaflet distribution, door to door canvassing, deputations, collections, etc. While we received declarations of sympathy I do not think it can be said that opposition to the Poll Tax reached the dimension of being a mass movement. It certainly never came near to the mass involvement that I had witnessed in the St. Pancras rent strike that I have already covered. It may be that in St. Pancras we were fighting Borough Council, whereas the Poll Tax had an apparently all-powerful Government behind it.

Nevertheless, throughout the country there was massive latent resistance to the Tax. This is clear from the very large number of people everywhere who either did not pay at all or who quite calmly allowed themselves to get into heavy arrears. There were others who concealed themselves from the local authorities by not registering on the electoral roll. It was thought that that particular tactic might have the not intended result of losing Labour some seats in the 1992 General Election. But, overall, it had the positive outcome of getting rid of Mrs. Thatcher as Prime Minister. Tory M.P's began to realise that the Poll Tax was a vote loser and they ganged up to replace her with the 'softer face' of John Major. There was another quite tangible plus to the campaign: Michael Heseltine, the new minister responsible for the Tax, allocated nearly £150 a head to local authorities to keep the Tax down. We can say that we have won a partial victory.

Now, the Major Government is to replace the Poll Tax with something different. No doubt they will try to recover what they have lost. But they will have to be careful. The lessons of the Poll Tax campaign will remain in peoples' minds for some time.

Like many other campaigners I had refused to pay the tax and ended up in Highbury Court. The magistrate was a sly old bird who already knew every argument that could be presented. He started off in a quite affable manner and said something like this:

"If you just let me know that you accept that you have to pay I will only make a Liability Order against you. But if you want to make a protest and confine it to a short statement I will award additional costs of £50. However, if you are going to argue a case against the Poll Tax it will be £80."

The 40 people in the dock chose one or other of these three categories. Naturally, I had thought quite a lot about what position I should take up: I was against the Poll Tax but not against the Islington Borough Council who were the statutory body responsible for raising the Tax and who were dependent on it for providing services. To my mind it was important to make a statement that distinguished between the two authorities. This put me in the third category of plaintiffs. I didn't relish having an additional £80 marked up against me. But it had to be. I started off:

"I am not against Islington Council. I think it is a very good Council. It is the Tory Government I am against..."

I wasn't allowed to say another word. "Sit down! SIT DOWN" shouted the old boy. His class instinct was as good as mine, only we were on opposite sides of the divide.

Pictures: (top left) Alec with Duncan, Ruthie and Jock; (centre left) in uniform; (bottom left) election talk with activists; (top right) Bridget making a wall hanging; (centre right) Bridget and Jock; (bottom right) viewing the Don Cook memorial plaque

Chapter 11 - What Would I do Without Her?

I sometimes ask myself how it is that Bridget and I have remained so close throughout over 50 years married life. One of the things that make that question interesting is that we come from such different backgrounds. Bridget was from a family of Jewish intellectuals. Her father was a very well known German demographer with an international reputation, and her mother an artist. The family left Germany when Hitler came to power. Her elder brother is also internationally known as a Marxist economist, and probably the most prolific writer in the GDR on a wide range of subjects. An elder sister – code-named Sonya – had an adventurous life in China and Japan alongside Richard Sorge, the famous Soviet agent who advised Stalin of the impending Nazi attack on the Soviet Union. Sonya was decorated by the Soviets for her work. In the second half of her life she became a much respected writer in the GDR. Bridget, herself, had a degree in History at Basle University. Of course, all this I did not know until well after we were married.

I met Bridget at a Communist Party residential school in the summer of 1948. I fell for her immediately. It was not only her attractive appearance; there was something indefinable about her that captured me. Before then I did not have any serious relationships with girls. There were two in the Hamilton branch who sometimes came to tea at our house, and with whom I occasionally went for walks. But for me, that remained quite innocent and without commitment. With Bridget, from the first moment I set eyes on her it was different. In fact, during that week we were both at the school, I was so attentive to her that she began to take notice. I continued at the school after Bridget had left but we had made a date that I would call on her in London on my way home. That was my first weekend with Bridget. Then, over the next 18 months there were numerous visits to London by me and some to Scotland by Bridget. When we were not together hundreds of love letters were exchanged – it is from these that I've researched much of the information for this book.

Bridget had been married before and had two young children. The marriage had come to an end, but it was not possible for her to even think of moving to Scotland. There were the children; she had a good flat in London – and what that meant in those early post-war days of housing shortage! Besides, she was at that time engaged on a mammoth task of

What Would I Do Without Her?

compiling statistical tables for her recently deceased father's massive work _A Demographic Survey of the British Colonial Empire_. And there I was, a dedicated and loyal Party organiser 400 miles away. I decided that I should ask the Party for permission to give up my responsibilities in Lanarkshire and go to London. Here is what I wrote to Bridget:

"There is no half-way house. We must go the full way and face up to all these problems instead of hiding from them. You are the only woman I have ever thought about. That was why I hesitated that first night in London. I knew how I felt, but I was not fully certain about how you felt. It had to be, and must be, everything or nothing. I wouldn't want you to feel good just for a short time and then be more unhappy later."

I asked Bill Laughlan, then the Scottish Party secretary, for an interview. Here is how it went:

J.N: I would like to go to London. It is for personal reasons. I am raising this now for, if my request is agreed to, changes will have to be made fairly soon so that the comrades put in charge are familiar with the area in time for the Municipal and General Elections
B.L.:   What is your personal reason? Is it domestic?
J.N: No. (pause)
B.L: Is it a woman?
J.N: Yes.
B.L.:   Don't tell me you've got yourself involved in some 'trouble'
J.N   No. It is quite straightforward and honest.
B.L: (long pause) Well, you'd better put your request before the comrades. You should be prepared to give a full explanation, otherwise it will be very difficult for the comrades to understand.

Following my interview with Bill I wrote to the Scottish Committee:

"I have very strong personal reasons for wanting to live in London. It cannot be arranged otherwise, and I expect you will understand my position. I fully recognise my responsibility to the Party here, but I would like you to give consideration to my being transferred to London, where I would put myself at the disposal of the District Committee there, either for work in industry or wherever else it may be decided..."

Over the next few weeks there was a lot more discussion in the Scottish leadership about my request than I had ever anticipated. One of the problems they were thinking about at that time was the situation in Fife where Willie Gallacher had been Communist MP since 1935. We were now at a high point in the Cold War and it was recognised that extraordinary measures needed to be taken to hold the seat. A decision had already been taken to send in a couple of additional full-timers to help galvanise the Party in Fife. My request had served to push this item further up the agenda. Three names were already being considered, but none of them had as good a grip of the mining situation as I had, and as Fife was predominantly a mining area, there now appeared an answer to both questions: this took the form that I would be transferred to Fife until the General Election, then I would be free to move to London. In the end this amounted to nearly a year and a half's separation for Bridget and me.

Plenty of passionate love affairs fizzle out. Not ours. I think there are a number of reasons. One was the so obvious warmth and affection Bridget had for the children. It followed quite naturally that she was the one who took charge of their health, education and welfare. I know the same thing happens in many marriages, but it was part of Bridget's 'being' that I admired.

Another thing was the competence with which she tackled the problems that came up in our domestic life. At one stage we were confronted with a serious housing problem. The Church Commissioners who owned the block of houses where we lived decided to put the property on the market. This could have had serious consequences for us; at least it would have meant a lengthy dislocation of our pattern of life while we were looking for other accommodation. But Bridget immediately got involved in the business.

She consulted lawyers and others and ultimately obtained a favourable mortgage from Camden Council, then along with another tenant took the initiative in getting a Housing Association formed. In the end, each tenant became a house-owner, with a repayment that was lower in nearly every case than the previous rent. These sentences amount to a great deal. It was easy for me to write them. But what a complex and difficult job it was to bring it about. I knew it was a task that was far beyond my abilities though I didn't think of it quite as consciously as that at the time. Rather, it grew on me that Bridget was much more than an equal partner in our marriage. I did not feel resentful. I came to respect and admire those qualities and abilities of Bridget that I knew I did not possess myself.

As often happens, good luck can change. In the course of the next few years some of the houses in the Association changed hands and were taken over by young upwardly mobile professionals. This was in the mid-80s, the years of 'Thatcherite yuppiedom'. They thought the boom-time would last forever. Property values were soaring. They saw their house as not a roof over their head but as a growing investment. They were ambitious and pushy. They wanted the property refurbished and modernised. It would add to their value. It had to be done in style. An ordinary builder wouldn't do. One of the Queen's builders was chosen to do the work. Dry rot was discovered. This added to the cost. The estimate amounted to £12,000 for each household.

I remember attending the Association meeting where all this was decided. Bridget had resigned as secretary some time earlier when she saw the way the wind was blowing. What was now being said was alarming. We were both retired. £12,000 would have eaten up every penny we had. And there was a young man snapping his fingers "£12,000 – that's peanuts!" he said. At that moment we knew we had to be on the move.

Actually, we were not really unlucky. We had no difficulty in selling and moved to a more proletarian area. We are quite happy with our new place. It is only ten minutes walk to Hampstead Heath. And from the transaction we gained a bit that has come in useful in supplementing our old age pensions.

That business happened only five years ago. The Thatcher boom is no more. Instead there is the recession. Property values have slumped and some of the yuppies don't even have a job. And even though they had the Queen's builders, dry rot has come back again to plague them.

I look at all this and say to myself: it was Bridget who piloted us away from these dangerous waters. You will see I have good reason for admiring my captain.

At every turn a new Bridget appears. Much earlier than I have just been talking about, her job at the Romanian Trade Office had come to an end and she moved to the Russian Bank. She decided to learn Russian – she already was fluent in German, English and French. I was knocked over by the dedication with which she tackled the new language. After doing a trying day's work and attending to the children's' needs she would settle down in her room for three or four hours concentrated study. For these sessions I drew a cartoon and tacked it up on her door. It showed a terrified child entering the room walking on his hands with the caption 'TOTAL SILENCE'. The children soon got the point that she must not be disturbed. I think this was the only time in their life that they approached her with some trepidation. Needless to say, Bridget soon became quite competent in that very difficult language.

One more example. One year we decided to take a holiday in Italy. Italian was a language that Bridget had never studied. A week or two before we were due to leave she bought an Italian phrase book and when we got there she had no difficulty in making herself understood. It was mainly things like that that strengthened my awareness that I was married to one much more gifted than myself.

All her adult life, Bridget has held one position or another in her Party branch. It would be secretary, or treasurer, or responsibility for literature sales. Whatever job she was doing she was sure to apply originality and fresh ideas. One example was the Marx-Engels walks she organised to raise money for the party branch. This involved preparing an itinerary of the various places of interest associated with Marx or Engels. This was never done in a routine way. It meant researching new information. As well as being a good money-raiser, the walks had a cultural and educational value. They were advertised in papers like the *New Statesman*, *Time Out*, and the *Morning Star* as well as in the locals, and attracted students and academics, many from overseas, in addition to people from various schools of Marxist thought.

By 1976 all the children had left home and I was earning for the first time, enough to cover our modest lifestyle. We agreed that it was time for Bridget to retire from paid employment and do the things that she had always wanted to do but never had the time. Very soon she was spending much of that time with *Labour Monthly*, on its editorial board and as one of its book reviewers. From 1976 till the magazine closed down in 1981 Bridget did a review practically every month as well as the occasional translation of an article from German into English for its columns.

Labour Monthly had a good reputation in the book trade because of the high standard of its reviews. It had plenty of good reviewers to call on, and being a monthly magazine the reviews were not a rush job, but rather more in the nature of studies. That was certainly the case with Bridget's reviews. How often she burned the midnight oil analysing, probing and researching sources. Here are a few of the titles she covered: *Karl Marx and World Literature* by SS Prawer; *Literature, the Individual and Society* by Raymond Southall; *Decay and Renewal* by Jack Lindsay; *Literary Presentations of a Divided Germany* by Peter Hutchinson; *The Novel and the People* by Ralph Fox; and many others.

I have an admission to make. Throughout our married life Bridget has often been unfaithful to me. How often have I been a bit resentful when all evening she wrapped herself around a book and had neither eyes nor words for me. Then, when it was time for bed, the following exchange would take place:

J.N.   It's midnight. I'm off to bed. Are you coming?
B.N.   In a minute. I'll just finish this page.

A couple of hours later

J.N.   Look at the time. Two o'clock. I thought you were coming.
B.N.   Soon. Only a couple of pages to finish this chapter,

Four o'clock

J.N.   Christ wumman! Are you never coming?!
B.N.   Stop pestering me. I've nearly finished the book.

A curious thing happened around that time. Bridget and I had been away on an outing and when we arrived back home we discovered there had been a break-in at our flat. The mortise lock had been forced but there was very little damage to the woodwork. It was obviously an expert job. Strangely, there was little disorder; some drawers had been left partly open. At first we couldn't find anything missing. It seemed that we had disturbed the intruder before he had an opportunity to ransack the place. But how had he got past us? Not on the stairs. Not out of the window for we were three floors up, and anyway, all the windows remained shut and latched. We called in the police but they couldn't solve the mystery either.

It was sometime later that we discovered one item had gone. It was a heavy gold medallion embossed with Cyrillic lettering, which had been presented to employees of the Moscow Narodny Bank on the 50th anniversary of the opening of its London branch. It was too long a shot to jump to the conclusion that it had been a MI5 job. But one thing pointed to that possibility. At the beginning of the war, Bridget had been working at the BBC Listener Research when one day she was called into the office and told that her contract was terminated as of that moment and she must leave the building immediately. No explanation was given. It was only when the Peter Wright book was published revealing just how wide was the scale of MI5 break-ins that my suspicion was confirmed. I wonder if the British Government will ever allow the same access to their files that they have succeeded in obtaining from the KGB If so, they can keep the gold medallion. It might help with the balance of payments problem.

I know from hundreds of conversations that all her life the person whom Bridget most respected – no, adored – was her father, the academic, the intellectual. Now, something strange has happened. It is as though her mother is demanding to be recognised. In her 70s a new Bridget exists; it is Bridget the artist. Up until recently I thought of her as one who could hardly draw a straight line. Now she is Bridget of scores of batik creations and patchwork designs. Our own flat now says so many different things: relaxing soft coloured curtains and fierce batik wall coverings.

Who is this strange person I have for a wife? An alarming conversation we had the other day: which one of us will die first? Jocularly, she said: why, of course, ladies first. I am depressed. What a terrible thought. What a void without Bridget.

It is just two days since I wrote that last paragraph. Yesterday I had to see the consultant at the hospital. For nearly a year I had what I thought to be a memory problem. I had been in the Hospital for Nervous Diseases where they carried out all kinds of tests only to tell me that they could find nothing abnormal. Then three weeks ago when I was driving Bridget home from her batik class I had a blackout and crashed into a wall. It has made me very nervous. There is something wrong with me. It is not just memory, it is physical. Now it had been arranged for me to see the consultant again. As the time for the interview approached I became increasingly agitated and short tempered. In that distorted state of mind I thought Bridget was showing more interest in her batik exhibition than in my condition. I exploded with cruel words. The result: I saw the consultant alone – without Bridget. Never had I so much needed her to lean on for comfort. But there was no Bridget.

Now, the pattern of both our lives has changed completely. I can no longer drive or fetch Bridget from her classes or exhibitions. Her activities will be severely curtailed. Nor will we be able to visit all those remote places in Scotland that we had planned for this summer. And if the temptation is too much for me and I venture into a fast stream to cast a fly to a rising trout and have a blackout it will be an end like Robert Maxwell's. The autopsy will be unable to determine whether it was due to natural causes or...

Postscript

Bridget died on March 17th 1997 at the Royal Free Hospital in London, following an operation. Mark, Jose and I were at her bedside at the end.

All you have read so far in this manuscript was written by 1992. I sent the manuscript to a few left-wing publishers and got encouraging replies, but no more than that. The manuscript was put away into a drawer and taken out only on rare occasions.

What you are now about to read is being written at the beginning of 2007 on my 85th birthday. It is ten years since Bridget died and you may recall that I was weighed down by a feeling of sadness and despair. How did I overcome this feeling? For a start I wrote *Bridget and Me,* which was a celebration of her life and her many achievements. But as time passed what else did I do to fill in my time? I joined the Walthamstow Fly-fishers Club and enjoyed the camaraderie of its members. Now I am too frail for fishing and have put away my rods.

But don't feel sorry for me for I have so many friends who visit me - too many to name though I must make an exception for Penny and David B who do so much for me.

I said Bridget had died. I should modify that statement. I see bits of her in Rosa and Louise. Their dedication and determination to achieve what they set out to do. I see it especially in Jose. Here I am pondering and dithering about one of those problems that come up in every-day life and Jose arrives, picks up the phone and sorts out the problem. They are all 'do-ers'!

Now at 85 years of age I know I am moving towards the end of a turbulent life. I do not have any fears or anxiety about this, I know it has been a worthwhile life and with lots of enjoyment as well.

On one of my living room walls I have a large panel of photographs taken on different holidays. I think we visited every country in Europe for long stretches at a time, and travel was always free thanks to concessions won by the union.

Every night before going to bed I look at these photos and say to Bridget: "Didn't we have an enjoyable life, as well as a turbulent life!"